Understanding Misunderstanding

Locke Holds the Key

Terence Moore

Published by

MELROSE BOOKS

An Imprint of Melrose Press Limited
St Thomas Place, Ely
Cambridgeshire
CB7 4GG, UK
www.melrosebooks.co.uk

FIRST EDITION

Cover designed by Melrose Books

ISBN 978-1-910792-94-0
epub 978-1-910792-95-7
mobi 978-1-910792-96-4

Printed and bound in Great Britain by:
Berforts South West Limited
17 Burgess Road
Hastings
East Sussex
TN35 4NR

Dedication

For Chris who without doubt made this a better book

Acknowledgements

In addition to Chris Carling, whose ideas and suggestions undoubtedly made this a better book, I am also greatly indebted to three individuals. The first is the editor of eight volumes of Locke's correspondence, E. S. de Beer (OUP, 1976). Letters can be revealing. Locke's letters reveal the man behind the philosopher, the politician, the Christian, the economist and the educationist. It was that man I was trying to find. Beer helped me find him.

The second scholar was Maurice Cranston. His masterly biography *John Locke*, (OUP, 1985) too addressed the man and his relationships, particularly his very special relationship with Damaris Masham, née Cudworth. Cranston pointed me towards the significance of the poems they had written to each other at an early stage in their relationship. Locke signed himself as 'Philander', Damaris appeared as 'Philoclea'.

The third individual is the editor of *Think* – a journal of the Royal Institute of Philosophy – the philosopher Stephen Law. Stephen's contribution was a rare gift: encouragement. He sought, from contributors to *Think,* papers that were 'engaging and accessible'. Earlier versions of nine of the conversations in this book first appeared in volumes of *Think*, starting in the summer of 2004. To know that they all satisfied his criteria was hugely encouraging.

There are others to whom I am indebted, too many to name, who at various times in various places commented helpfully on talks I gave over the years on Locke, language and understanding. I would also like to record my debt to Peter H. Nidditch. I returned time and time again to his edition of *An Essay Concerning Human Understanding* (OUP, 1975) and made use of it in these conversations, invariably gaining from his scholarship.

CONTENTS

Introduction

John Locke's *An Essay Concerning Human Understanding* is one of philosophy's major classics, taking its place among the pantheon of Western thought. All the more surprising then, for a work so well-known, that some of Locke's most far-reaching and original ideas in the *Essay* have been widely ignored. Book III, entitled *Of Words or Language in General*, offers fresh and radical insights into the basic workings of language: how we understand one another, why we misunderstand one another, what the links are between words and meanings. And yet these insights have been largely overlooked by scholars more interested in his thoughts on the grounds of knowledge and his alleged empiricism.

This book aims to bring Locke's ideas about language out of the darkness and into the light. Not by explaining his views but by letting Locke speak for himself. It occurred to me that one of the reasons Locke's linguistic insights had not changed the way we look at words and meanings was the 17th century idiom of his writing. One of his key ideas, for instance, he called 'Secret Reference' – a phrase not at all easy to fathom, yet one with mind-changing significance.

I have a picture of Locke, painted by the leading portrait artist of the time, Godfrey Kneller, in my room in Old Court, Clare College, Cambridge. Looking at this portrait one day, I suddenly thought: *suppose Locke spoke in modern English. Suppose, in the language of Star Trek, I beamed Locke up to my room and we engaged in conversations about his ideas in the language of today. Might that be the way to reveal the communal conspiracy underlying 'Secret Reference' and bring Locke's originality to light?*

And so the conversations were born. This book brings together ten linked conversations between myself, Terence Moore, theoretical linguist, Fellow of Clare and John Locke, distinguished 17th century philosopher, Fellow of Christ Church, Oxford. Our conversations are wide-ranging as we discuss and explore Locke's ideas on language, understanding and misunderstanding. Readers in a hurry will, after reading conversations one and two on 'Secret Reference', discover three of the leading ideas driving the book. Namely: Words do not contain meanings. Words spark meanings in the mind. Minds differ.

A further benefit of beaming Locke up to my room is that he now has the run of my library and so is able to engage with modern thinkers and poets – Chomsky, Orwell, Eliot, for instance – comparing his ideas on language with theirs, seeing how far his insights have stood the test of time.

Was Book III on Language an Afterthought?

One of the reasons Book III of the *Essay* has not been given the attention it deserves may be because Locke himself did not originally intend to write it. The *Essay* itself, four books, is an enquiry into the grounds of knowledge. Locke explores concepts such as 'Idea', analysing 'Types of Idea', asking how do we know what we know? As the enquiry progressed, however, and being a man of fundamentals, Locke came to see that in order to discuss the concept 'Idea', he had to use words. Therefore, to keep the enquiry grounded, he needed to explore the nature of meaning. Not just how do we know what we know, but how do we represent what we know to ourselves through language, and how do we express what we believe we know so that others will understand us? As it turned out this further exploration did not come easily. In a letter to a friend he admitted that Book III had cost him 'more pains' than any of the others. There is, I believe, a note of weariness at the end of Book II at having to take up the wrestle with words and meanings. He writes:

> I find there is so close a connection between *Ideas* and words ... that it is impossible to speak clearly and distinctly of our Knowledge, which all consists in Propositions, without considering, first the Nature, Use and Signification of Language; which must therefore be the business of the next Book.

Who was John Locke?

We are inclined to think of the great intellects of the past as pure minds. We explore the legacy of their minds more than their lives. Interestingly the epitaph Locke wrote for himself in Latin, once in the churchyard of All Saints, High Laver, Essex, now in the church itself, seems to encourage the view that the mind matters more than the man. Cranston's paraphrase runs:

> Stay Traveller.
> Near this place lies John Locke. If you wonder what kind of man he was, the answer is that he was one contented with his modest lot. A scholar by training, he devoted his studies wholly to the pursuit of truth. Such you may learn from his writings ... His vertues, if he had any, were too slight to serve either to his own credit or as an example to you. Let his vices be interred with him. As an example of vertue you have already in the Gospels; an example of vice one could wish did not exist; an example of mortality (and may you learn from it) you have assuredly here and everywhere. That he was born on August 29, 1632, and died on October 28, 1704, this tablet, which itself will quickly perish, is a record.

The reality of Locke's life, however, was very different. Though the epitaph paints a picture of Locke as an academic spending his life in quiet contemplation, in fact nothing could be further from the truth. Though starting his professional life as a Fellow of Christ Church, Oxford, a chance encounter with the most powerful statesman in the land at that time, the Earl of Shaftesbury, resulted in Locke being caught up with the political and religious turbulence of those years. The issues dividing the land were not trivial but quite literally matters of life and death. He once recalled: 'I no sooner perceived myself in the world but I found myself in a storm which has lasted almost hitherto.'

A Century of Political and Religious Turbulence

During Locke's lifetime, a country in which power had rested largely and by divine right in the hands of a monarch was slowly becoming a country with a sovereign parliament. The shift from royal absolutism and royal prerogative to a constitutional monarchy and parliamentary sovereignty was slow and often lethal to both sides – royalists and parliamentarians.

A 17-year-old Locke was close by in Westminster School, a royalist stronghold, the momentous day at the climax of the Civil War when a King, Charles I, was beheaded. England's Civil War had begun a decade after Locke was born. The Civil War was probably the most lethal conflict England ever suffered, estimates of the dead suggesting around 86,000 soldiers were killed in the fighting. Those losses, in a population of four to five million, were proportionately much higher than those England suffered in the First World War, another bloody conflict. Locke then lived through Cromwell's brief republic, the Commonwealth, then the restoration of a second King, Charles II. Charles, on his death, was succeeded by his brother James, a Catholic in a country growing evermore Protestant. James was eventually ousted, fleeing to France after the Glorious Revolution of 1688.

Locke and the 17th Century

Little of this political and religious turbulence might have touched Locke had he remained in what some people may think of as an ivory tower – his college rooms in Christ Church, Oxford – pursuing philosophical questions. The unexpected twist to his fortunes came by way of that chance encounter with Shaftesbury, an encounter which seems to have satisfied a deep need in Locke. During the winter of 1656, Locke, aged 24, had written a moving letter to a friend in his home village of Pensford, Somerset. He longed, he wrote, for a pilot in life: 'Oh for a pilot who would steer this tossed ship … into a haven of happiness.'

Ten years later he had his wish granted, or at least half of it. The pilot Locke longed for appeared in the person of Shaftesbury, eminent statesman, Chancellor of the Exchequer, then Lord High Chancellor, but not to steer him to a haven of happiness. Locke's pilot was to guide him not into, but out of, a safe haven and into very stormy seas indeed.

If it was by chance Locke found himself swept into the orbit of the most powerful statesman in the land, he did not resist. Indeed he appears to have relished finding his destiny for more than fifteen years linked with a man at the centre of the fierce controversies around the King, Charles II, his religious beliefs and the extent of his authority. Whilst the meeting with Shaftesbury happened by pure chance, the resulting friendship was momentous and deeply formative for Locke. It opened his mind, channelled his intellectual energies and eventually led to his great works, including *Two Treatises on Government* and *An Essay Concerning Human Understanding*, (particularly Book III of the *Essay*, *Of Words or Language in General*).

When Locke first met Shaftesbury he was a little-known Oxford don, living in Christ Church, a minor scholar, an unqualified physician, an unpublished writer and an amateur scientist. Shortly after their meeting, Locke left his rooms in the college and moved into Shaftesbury's home, Exeter House, in London on the Strand. In the heady atmosphere of Exeter House, Locke became politically active, a radical by the standards of the day, helping Shaftesbury in his drive to rein in the King's power by increasing the authority of Parliament. In short, Locke, the close friend, became Shaftesbury's right-hand man and a first-rate mini-Civil Service, writing his speeches, developing his political, religious, economic policies, and as a Commissioner of Trade, appointed by Shaftesbury, helping draft his Constitution for the newly-created province of Carolina.

Their daily engagement with using language to persuade must have seen them arguing about words and meanings, recognising they did not always understand each other. Together they considered their audience, trying to assess how far their listeners and readers might understand, half-understand, misunderstand their words. All this meant Locke could draw on a wealth of linguistic experience of diverse modes of communicating when later he set out on his own enquiry into the 'Nature, Use and Signification of Language.'

A Century of Genius?

According to A.N.Whitehead, the 17th century was 'the century of genius'. Whitehead had good reasons – this was the time of Newton, Boyle, Bacon, Wren, Harvey and of course Locke. Moreover it was also the century that saw the emergence of the Royal Society, founded to discuss a new philosophy – to promote knowledge of the material world through observation, experiment, testable explanations and predictions. Its full title catches its aims: The Royal Society for the Improving of Natural Knowledge. Its motto catches its spirit: 'Nullius in Verba'. Roughly paraphrased, 'Take Nobody's Word for it'. The motto captures the determination of the Fellows to reject the unreflective commitment to tradition and to replace it with appeals to the consequences of observation and experiment. Locke, one of the early Fellows of the Royal Society relished what we might call 'the scientific approach'.

It is clear that Locke straddled both sides of the 17th century – its genius and its turbulence. Being embroiled in its turbulence was to lead eventually to a royalist warrant out for Locke's arrest, to his fleeing to Holland in1683, going into hiding, changing his name, becoming Dr van der Linden, to being expelled from his royalist college, Christ Church. A consequence of being so embroiled meant that Locke did not return to England till after the Glorious Revolution of 1688, the year that saw William and Mary ascend the throne. Even after his return, the Heads of Oxford Colleges passed a resolution to suppress his *An Essay Concerning Human Understanding.*

All this meant that Locke's genius, his reflections on words, meanings, language and understanding in Book III of the *Essay*, were not the work of a quiet academic in an Oxford College, aloof from the bloody arena of political life. His ideas on language were fostered by his involvement with the political life in Exeter House. Locke was very much of the world, making his ideas pertinent – highly pertinent – to our use of language today. We can learn, for example, from Locke's analysis of 'Secret Reference', how we might develop better ways of communicating with each other – ways likely to reduce the chances of our half-understanding or being half-understood, our listeners assuming they know what we mean when their understanding can't help but be partial. Indeed a recurring theme in Book III is the inherent indeterminacy of the meanings of words. Perhaps the most persuasive reason for engaging with Locke's linguistic ideas is that they raise our awareness of the limitations of language, of the obstacles that stand in the way of our understanding one another. 'Secret Reference' reveals to us the extent to which we overestimate the power of language to express ourselves clearly. We therefore fail to recognise the way understanding is a matter of degree. Much of the time we only understand one another up to a point. These conversations with Locke help us to see why.

As Locke puts it: 'The greatest part of the Questions and Controversies that perplex Mankind depend on the doubtful and uncertain use of Words.'

Welcome to my room!

Conversation One

'The greatest part of the Questions and Controversies that perplex Mankind depend on the doubtful and uncertain use of Words.'

Locke: 'The Epistle to the Reader'
An Essay Concerning Human Understanding

Secret Reference: Locke's Key to Meaning

In their first conversation, the beamed-up John Locke addresses Terence Moore's unease over the fragility of our understanding of each other's language. As Moore puts it, our experience of using language is invariably mixed. Sometimes language works: we appear to be understood. Sometimes it doesn't: we appear to be misunderstood. Why the constant oscillation between understanding and misunderstanding? Why in particular is misunderstanding so rife?

An original and radical answer emerges as Moore and Locke discuss Locke's analysis of the underpinnings of language use, the nature of meaning and the limits to our understanding of each other's words. Locke's answer first establishes the ultimate privacy of our meanings – a privacy that entails our need to engage in a tacit, communal conspiracy to be able to communicate at all. The key to that conspiracy he calls 'Secret Reference'. As the conversation progresses we begin to see more clearly why 'Secret Reference' matters to us today.

Moore: Let's plunge straight in. What exactly did you mean by 'Secret Reference'? How does it explain the necessarily provisional and uncertain nature of our understanding of each other and of the world?

Locke: I'm not sure plunging in is wise. Wouldn't it be better if I spelt out the fundamental problem I saw 'Secret Reference' as a solution to? Then we can follow through its implications for our understanding of each other's language.

Moore: Of course, you're right. I'm always jumping ahead of myself. The fundamental problem 'Secret Reference' addresses has to be your weird and radical view of meaning, doesn't it? You argue that words have no meanings. That can't be right, can it? Everybody knows words have meanings. It's common sense.

Locke: Common sense can be wrong. Common sense says the sun rises and the sun sets. But we know it does no such geocentric thing. Anyway, surely I didn't exactly say words have no meaning.

Moore: True, it was me who said it. What you said in Chapter III, Book III was words 'would be Signs of nothing, Sounds without Signification.'

Locke: I added though that words have no meaning until each of us individually creates a meaning for ourselves by filtering public words through complex private processes in our heads.

Moore: You certainly never said that in *An Essay Concerning Human Understanding*!

Locke: Maybe not those words exactly. But it's what I had in mind.

Moore: You're saying that's what you had in mind when you said repeatedly in Book III that 'Words in their primary or immediate Signification, stand for nothing, but the Ideas in the mind of him that uses them'.

Locke: It's not very 21st century language, is it? Let me try to recast it in your idiom. Perhaps I should say something like: the meanings of the words we use depend upon each of us creating for ourselves links between public words and private ideas in our own heads.

Moore: So I'm to understand words are meaningless unless each of us makes those links for ourselves?

Locke: I do have to repeat myself, don't I? Yes, I'm saying words have no meaning until we each personally link them to ideas in our own heads, in our own way.

Moore: Alright, but convince me. Treat me as a naïve realist – someone who believes that the meanings of words are objects out there in the world, not here inside our heads – things to be pursued, hunted down platonically till we find the real, the true meaning.

Locke: The real, the true meaning! Poppycock! There's no such animal. Have I got that right? I like the sound of it – poppycock!

Moore: Poppycock? As a term for nonsense, yes. But why? Why is the naïve realist's view poppycock?

Locke: Because it rests on reifying meaning – treating meaning as a thing, an entity. Reifiers assume words contain meanings. They don't. Words can excite meanings in minds the way catalysts can excite chemical reactions. But the words themselves remain meaningless, empty husks. What words do have is potential – the power to excite ideas and feelings in the individual minds of people.

Moore: So 'Uttering a word is like striking a note on the keyboard of the imagination.'

Locke: You're quite the poet!

Moore: Not me, alas, Wittgenstein. Have the poets got it wrong then? Eliot, for instance:

> Words strain
> Crack and sometimes break, under the burden
> Under the tension, slip, slide, perish,
> Decay with imprecision, will not stay in place,
> Will not stay still.

Locke: Yes, literally Eliot is wrong, or better, confusing, as poets often are. It's not words that do any of those things. Words are actually pretty stable. Take 'wicked' for instance. Hasn't its meaning gone from 'bad' to 'good'?

Moore: Not for me yet!

Locke: Yet the word itself hasn't changed. It's the meanings of words that can crack, break, slip, slide … will not stay in place, will not stay still. Though actually, the more fundamental problem with this bit of Eliot is his unspoken assumption.

Moore: That somehow the meanings of words were once precise and need not slide, slip, decay with imprecision?

Locke: Exactly. Eliot must have had mathematics or logic in mind, not language. Language begins and ends in imprecision – though, fortunately, the degrees can vary.

Moore: I'm wavering, but I'm still not totally convinced. Why is Eliot, why are the reifiers, so very wrong to believe words contain meanings?

Locke: Consider some evidence. Let's do an experiment. Let's take a word that's meaningless to you and see what goes on when you try to create a meaning for it.

Moore: Alright. What word do you have in mind?

Locke: Let me try 'struthious'. What ideas does the word 'struthious' excite in your mind?

Moore: Absolutely none – never heard it before.

Locke: Good. So to you it's a meaningless word.

Moore: Meaningless yes, but syntactically quite rich. I'd guess it's an adjective like 'curious, or 'furious'. That its abstract noun might be 'struthiosity' or possibly 'struthy'. That the comparative form is likely to be 'more struthious', that …

Locke: Yes, yes. I know you were once a syntactician of the generative school, but I'm talking semantics. We can agree you recognise 'struthious' as a possible English word, technically an adjective, but it remains a word empty of meaning. To make it meaningful for you we have to take one giant stride for mankind.

Moore: Which is?

Locke: Invoke the mind. The mind is the great creator of meanings for each individual. Each mind takes the words it hears and annexes them to its own ideas of the world. Meanings emerge from the processes by which each individual mind fuses public words with their private ideas.

Moore: So you're saying meanings are basically mind-dependent.

Locke: It's not the whole story, but mind-dependent will do for starters. Let's see what bundle of ideas the word 'struthious' might knot together for you.

Moore: Is this your strand theory of meaning?

Locke: Strand theory of meaning! I never used that expression in the *Essay*. But I like it. It strikes a note on the keyboard of my imagination!

Moore: 'Strands' is a gloss I put upon your knot-and-bundle image of word and meaning – an image you return to several times in the *Essay*. You describe the word as a knot tying bundles of ideas together. One example I remember was the word 'courage'. That bundle had five or six strands:

'perceiving danger', 'presence of fear', 'not being affected by the fear', 'careful consideration of what needs to be done', 'carrying out the appropriate action'.

Locke: It's true, I do see words acting like knots tying together strands of meaning, even if I didn't express it exactly like that. The nub of the problem with communicating is that while we may share the word, the knot, we may not share the bundle of meaning, the strands of ideas, it ties together. Some strands we may share, some we may not. Going back to 'struthious', I have a number of strands and you at the moment have none.

Moore: None as yet. I'm hoping to pick some up.

Locke: Suppose I put the word to work in a sentence. Taking language out of its context of use, as Saussure – your acclaimed Father of Modern Linguistics – did, has only a limited value. Let me tell you about a friend of mine, Max. Suppose I tell you that 'Max is struthious'.

Moore: That tells me absolutely nothing about him!

Locke: So far that's true. Suppose I tell you the ideas 'struthious' excite for me revolve around ostriches.

Moore: Ostriches!

Locke: Ostriches.

Moore: So you're telling me Max is ostrich-like?

Locke: Does that tell you anything about Max?

Moore: It tells me something about your view of Max. You think he's reluctant to face unpleasant things – he's an in-the-sand head-burier.

Locke: Yes, that's an aspect of Max's behaviour I've observed several times. Forget Max. Instead note how my ostrich clue started you pulling together some strands of meaning for 'struthious'. Not that I was sure you knew the fabled behaviour of ostriches.

Moore: Everybody knows the story about the way ostriches behave in face of danger.

Locke: Maybe, maybe not. Suppose you hadn't known the story. Knowing that the ideas 'struthious' excites for me concern ostriches wouldn't have been any sort of clue to what I had in mind when I commented on Max.

Moore: So?

Locke: Don't you see? In using language, I can never know for sure what experience, what beliefs, what initial conditions you bring to processing the words I use. I can assume, or guess, or imagine you know the sorts of things I know, but I can't be sure. In the end you have to filter my words through your mind and therefore the meanings you arrive at are your own meanings, not mine. The personal filtering is all. The fact you can't begin to understand the words I use until you have passed them through the filters of your own mind is what makes meanings ultimately mind-dependent, ultimately person-dependent.

Moore: So you're saying that I understand your words because I imagine they are mine. Or rather I imagine your meanings are the same as mine. You're reeling me in. I'm about ready to jettison the common sense view of meaning. When you wrote in Book III, 'Words in every Man's Mouth stand for the Ideas he has, and which he would express by them', was that a declaration of the private, subjective nature of meaning – that our strands were our own property?

Locke: A declaration! No. More my attempt to say something about where meaning is localised – in the head. Looking back I realise I should have talked more about the process, the filtering process. The absolute necessity to filter words through our own minds spells out why it is each of us can apply a word only to his own bundle of ideas, not to somebody else's.

Moore: Actually you did say that in the same paragraph: 'it is evident that each can apply the word only to his own Ideas, nor can he make it stand as a Sign of such a complex Idea, as he has not.'

Locke: Bit long-winded, but it does hammer home the basic idea. The origins of meanings for words depend in the end on intricate processes in individual minds – processes I could only speculate on.

Moore: Setting aside the processes in the brain – which we in the 21st century are still largely ignorant about too – let me acknowledge I'm convinced. Meanings, I'll agree, are in the last resort mind-dependent. However, I have another problem. I think you're inconsistent.

Locke: Inconsistent! Where?

Moore: On the one hand you claim our meanings for words are ultimately private, yet you also claim language is, let me get the quote right, 'the great Instrument and common Tye of Society'. How can it be either of those things if we are all semantic individualists with our own meanings locked in our own heads?

Locke: Because we fool ourselves. We hold something to be true, which is not true but which it is sublimely useful to believe is true. In short we 'secretly refer'.

Moore: Now we get to it! 'Secret Reference'. Your solution to the problem created by the essentially personal and subjective nature of the meanings of our words. Your highly individual key to understanding how we understand one another!

Locke: Indeed. Let me try to explain. As you have kindly pointed out, I repeatedly insist words as we use them can properly and immediately signify only our own ideas …

Moore: The ultimate privateness of our strands of meanings.

Locke: … Nevertheless, if you recall, I add an escape clause. Each of us, I believe, secretly refers – or better perhaps in an idiom that will seem less archaic, tacitly imagines – two fundamental things. I call these tacit acts of the imagination 'Secret Reference'.

Moore: So there are two kinds of 'Secret Reference'?

Locke: Yes but let's stick with the first 'Secret Reference' for the moment. What I believe we universally do is secretly imagine, or as you modern thinkers would probably prefer to say, tacitly imagine, that the words we're using excite the same ideas in the minds of others as they do in ours. That's what I had in mind when I said in Chapter II, Book III, we 'suppose our Words to be Marks of Ideas in the Minds of others, with whom we communicate'.

Moore: You're saying when we talk or write we're supposing – tacitly – that the meanings of our words are the same for others as they are for us?

Locke: That's right. Take now. I'm tacitly imagining my words are marking the same meanings in your mind as they are in mine. A bit rash, but that's what I'm doing!

Moore: So the first 'Secret Reference', or tacit act of the imagination, establishes the belief that our meanings are uniform across speakers. But it's not true.

Locke: Of course it's not true. How could it be? We've already agreed first, that to arrive at meanings for words we have to process them through our own heads. And second, that the strands knotted by words will differ to some degree at least for each of us. Nevertheless if we didn't tacitly imagine our strands of meaning were the same we would, as I remarked in the *Essay*, 'talk in vain, and could not be understood if the Sounds we applied to one Idea were such as by the Hearer were applied to another'. The need to make contact is the fundamental reason driving our innumerable, daily acts of 'Secret Reference'. We have little choice, beyond becoming Trappist monks.

Moore: So language, 'the great Instrument and common Tye of Society', is built upon something we imagine to be true, but it isn't – in short it's a lie!

Locke: Don't be so moralistic! 'The great Instrument and common Tye' is built upon a tacit, working hypothesis – a mostly unacknowledged hypothesis, I admit. But I'll acknowledge it. I'm now supposing you're understanding my words in the same way as I understand them. And to some degree I'm sure you are. Though our strands may differ, the meanings of our words do often overlap. The real trouble – the cancer at the heart of language – lies with the tacitness of the understanding. Ordinarily we just don't acknowledge, even to ourselves, what is going on as we talk. And it's the failure to acknowledge that can have fatal consequences for our understanding of each other and of the world.

Moore: For instance?

Locke: Let me give you two 'for instances'. First, once I imagine – however tacitly – that my meanings are your meanings, I don't need to check, to find out whether what you've understood by what I said is what I had in mind. Rather than checking we have similar strands, I, as speaker, simply assume you're understanding my words and their meanings. Could be a disastrous assumption – a recipe for misunderstanding!

Moore: Made worse since I, as hearer, rarely challenge you to tell me about your strands of meanings!

Locke: Absolutely! Checking and challenging are THE essential tools for establishing a degree of understanding.

Moore: What's the second instance?

Locke: Failing to acknowledge the role of 'Secret Reference' allows us to believe what your naïve realist believes: that the meanings of the words we're using are not ideas in our heads but somehow contained in the words themselves.

Moore: Rather than your way of putting it – what words do is excite meanings in our heads, in the way a lit fuse excites an explosion.

Locke: Yes. The container view paints a picture of communicating where words are, to use a simile from your time, like wagons in a goods train loaded with meanings shunting between me and you. Staying with the train metaphor, words should be seen as empty wagons, meaningless sounds, until, arriving at their destination, they ignite processes in the minds of those they were sent to.

Moore: I'm convinced we resolutely avoid acknowledging what's actually going on when we converse. I'm still not quite sure why nevertheless you still maintain language is 'the great Instrument and common Tye of Society'?

Locke: Sometimes I wonder why. Recall I never said language was an effective or necessarily efficacious instrument. Still, language does give us opportunities to try to understand each other. But I think you're right. I should have added that using language can also be dangerous – definitely a two-edged sword. One edge can hurt us; the other can enlighten us, particularly if we take on board the implications of 'Secret Reference'.

Moore: So you think even in our advanced day and age, when we've moved on hugely in so many fields since your 17th century, we should take on board your ancient idea of 'Secret Reference'?

Locke: The consequence of taking 'Secret Reference' on board is that we should erase from our use of language the question, 'What does that word mean?'

Moore: Because it's not the word that has meanings but the individual. I'm beginning to understand. Words don't mean. People mean things by way of words. Do you think we should have courses in our schools that explore the ways 'Secret Reference' underpins our use of language? Say, a course on the use of language and the pursuit of truth?

Locke: Have you forgotten, I did write a book entitled '*Some Thoughts on Education*', but I admit I didn't make language its focus? I think you're right though. It's in school that the ways language actually operates should be explored. Learning to check and challenge are basic skills best acquired early. I'd prefer a course title like, Language and the Pursuit of Understanding.

Moore: Better, I agree – covers both understanding the world and each other. To conclude, what's the appeal you derive from 'Secret Reference?

Locke: My reforming instinct is telling me to go for a homily. I'm tempted.

Moore: No homilies!

Locke: Just a brief one. We should remember – whenever the context demands it – the provisional and uncertain nature of the meanings for the words we use.

Moore: In a word their inherent indeterminacy.

Conversation Two

'It is a perverting the use of Words, and brings unavoidable Obscurity and Confusion whenever we make them stand for anything but those Ideas we have in our own Minds.'

Book III
An Essay Concerning Human Understanding

Locke's Second Secret Reference

Locke's second 'Secret Reference' complements the first in revealing another universal but tacit conspiracy we all collude in. This one is concerned with our tacit assumptions about the relation between language and the world of our experience. Not only do we act as if the meanings of the words we use are the same for others as they are for us, we further act as if, to use Locke's phrase, 'Words stand for the reality of Things.' We act, that is, as if there were a direct relation between language and the world. As if language were a nomenclature. What we fail once again to remember is that words, as Locke repeatedly insists, mark not things, but our ideas of 'the reality of Things.' If words aren't linked to ideas, Locke declares, they are nothing but so much 'insignificant Noise', sounds 'without Signification'.

Both 'Secret References' serve to underline the way our use of language relies on tacit assumptions that, whilst they remain unacknowledged, are a fertile source of misunderstanding.

Moore: In our first conversation we discussed the implications of your first 'Secret Reference' for any hope we can entertain of communicating successfully. But weren't there two 'Secret References' in Book III, two ways in which we act as if?

Locke: Definitely. And for me the second 'Secret Reference' is as important as the first. I'd go as far as to say it's one of the two great generators of the misuse and misunderstanding of language.

Moore: The other great generator of misunderstanding being your first 'Secret Reference'?

Locke: Of course.

Moore: I'm intrigued by your second 'Secret Reference'. It raises a number of questions for me. But I'm also intrigued by why it was that in *An Essay Concerning Human Understanding* you became so absorbed in problems of language, meaning and understanding.

Locke: I gave you my reasons at the end of Book II.

Moore: That's true. But the way you expressed it – it's almost as though analysing the fundamental workings of language was somewhat of an afterthought.

Locke: How so?

Moore: Well, after a very long detailed account of different sorts of ideas in Book II you conclude:

> I find there is so close a connexion between Ideas and Words, ... that it is impossible to speak clearly and distinctly of our Knowledge without considering, first, the Nature, Use, and Signification of Language, which must therefore be the business of the next book.

Don't you think you sound rather reluctant?

Locke: You're right. I suppose in a way I was reluctant. In the *Essay* I was exploring the grounds of knowing. I hadn't planned to write on language, forgetting I suppose that a great deal of our knowing is expressed in propositions, and propositions are made up of words. But what a difficult book to write! It cost me more pain than the other three put together!

Moore: It was worth it. For me it's the best book, the most insightful in the whole *Essay*. In particular in its emphasis on the subjective, ultimately private nature of meaning.

Locke: Yes, well after much soul-searching I realised there was no alternative but to delve into the underpinnings of language. The links between words and ideas is fundamental. As I say in the *Essay*: 'Words in their primary or immediate Signification, stand for nothing, but the Ideas in the Mind of him that uses them'.

Moore: Exactly. And you repeat that insight six or seven times in a chapter barely three pages long! So it was important to you, even though it does raise the fundamental question we discussed last time: how do we understand each other if our meanings for words are ultimately subjective, personal, private?

Locke: A question to which, as you know, I gave an answer: because we tacitly presuppose others have in mind the same meanings for the words we use as we have in our minds.

Moore: Your first 'Secret Reference'. Yes. It shows us all, without exception, as taking part in a tacit communal conspiracy.

Locke: The first 'Secret Reference' is an absolute tacit presupposition we all make. And it's useful as a working hypothesis. At the very least it launches the possibility of communicating, even if communication is not always successful.

Moore: But the second 'Secret Reference', the second tacit presupposition we all make. How does it relate to the first?

Locke: Well for a start both 'Secret References' conspire to hide the truth from us about how words in use actually work.

Moore: The first because, as you said, we tacitly presuppose that the words we use mean the same for others as they mean for us. But the second 'Secret Reference', what does that hide from us?

Locke: The second 'Secret Reference' hides from us the indirect relation between words and the world and has us believing that words stand for 'the reality of Things' when words actually stand for our ideas of 'the reality of Things'.

Moore: Yes, that's the way you put it when you first introduce the second 'Secret Reference'. Let me quote you because it's important: 'Secondly, Because Men would not be thought to talk barely of their own Imaginations, but of Things as they really are; therefore they often suppose their Words to stand also for the reality of Things.'

Locke: I suspect you would wish me to say, 'tacitly suppose' their words stand for 'the reality of Things'.

Moore: Only because it's more likely to excite in today's readers the ideas you have in mind. But that's not the important point is it?

Locke: No. The important point is that words generally don't and can't express the way things really are in any objective way. There is no direct link between words and the world, though we act as if there were.

Moore: Do you mean we tend to view language as a kind of naming process?

Locke: In a way.

Moore: Of course, there are words that do directly name entities in the world. Traditional grammarians would call them 'proper nouns'.

Locke: You mean the names of places, cities, mountains, rivers … where a single word or phrase is matched up by explicit agreement with a single city, or place or person in the world?

Moore: Yes, in the case of proper nouns there does seem to be a more direct link between words and the world.

Locke: Maybe so. But these are the exceptions rather than the rule. Most words stand for general categories. Think about it. 'Dog', 'car', 'computer', 'talk', 'run', 'laugh' … words like these stand for our ideas of a generalised 'dog', or 'act of laughter', which we may then use to mark specific examples.

Moore: I suppose that's right. Language can't really be a naming process. If it were, we'd need words to name every specific thing, action, event – we'd have to multiply by millions the number of words in the language. Our memories couldn't cope.

Locke: Absolutely. And yet we still tend to act as if our words reflect, not our ideas of how things are in the world, but the way things really are.

Moore: This brings us back to what I learned from you about meaning in our first conversation. Only a speaker or a listener can mean something by a word, the word itself is just a mark or a sound without inherent meaning. So how could it reveal to us 'the reality of Things'?

Locke: As I keep saying: 'It is a perverting the use of Words, and brings unavoidable Obscurity and Confusion whenever we make them stand for anything but those Ideas we have in our own Minds.'

Moore: And as I need to remember: 'Words in their primary or immediate Signification, stand for nothing, but the Ideas in the Mind of him that uses them'.

Locke: The second 'Secret Reference', to use your language, is the second tacit communal conspiracy we all collude in. It encourages us to suppose that the words we use stand directly for thing as they are. In truth, words about the world stand for things as we individually perceive them to be.

Moore: So if I have a word, say, 'happiness', it does not follow that I'm naming something existing out there in the world that we could search for and maybe find.

Locke: Of course not. What does follow is that you have ideas excited by the word 'happiness'. Though, as the first 'Secret Reference' tells us, they may not be the same ideas others have in mind.

Moore: So the two 'Secret References' do complement each other. Both are central to your enquiry into the nature, use and signification of language. The way they mislead us is that each, though differently, conceals from us the way words in use actually work.

Locke: I agree they work in tandem, both digging fertile ground for misunderstanding. The first would have us believe that the words we use excite the same thoughts and feelings in others as they do in us. Which they may or may not. The second would have us believe words can tell us about things as they are really.

Moore: Whereas, if I understand it, what you're saying is that because language in use is always mediated by ideas, and ideas are in individual minds, we can never be sure. There is, in effect, an inherent indeterminacy in our use of language.

Locke: That's it! On the nose. Our use is inherently, not accidentally, indeterminate.

Moore: But once we're on to the confusion both 'Secret References' can create, can't we begin to work at minimising the misunderstanding they cause? Can't we learn to work with the inherent indeterminacy of meanings? For example, in the case of the first 'Secret Reference' we could begin by starting to carefully check, where it matters, whether the thoughts and feelings our words have excited in others' minds are at all like the thoughts and feelings our words excite for us. As for the second 'Secret Reference', when controversies arise we can recall that the issue at stake is not the words themselves describing the world but the ideas of the world the words excite in individual minds.

Locke: We can minimise the consequences of the indeterminacy, yes. Eliminate, no.

Moore: Both 'Secret References' seem to hold our minds in a strong grip.

Locke: That's because we often appear to understand each other quite well. After all we share ideas and experience of living in the world. That helps. Think of it as the plus side of using language. Yet because of the influence of 'Secret Reference' we both overlook and overestimate the power of language. We forget that besetting our use of language is the inherent, not accidental, indeterminacy of our subjective meanings. And that has consequences.

Moore: I try not to forget!

Conversation Three

Locke's Belief: Morality is Demonstrable

In his *Essay* Locke makes an extravagant claim. He believes, he writes, 'Morality is demonstrable according to the mathematical method.' This belief – that whether some act is moral or not can be logically proved – is a textbook case of a thinker forgetting the implications of his own ideas. Moral judgements are expressed in words, and words according to Locke's insights in *An Essay Concerning Human Understanding* are marks of ideas in the different minds of the people conversing. The resulting indeterminacy at the heart of language in use makes Locke's claim about morality difficult to defend.

Though pressed by friends at the time (1690s), in particular his great Irish friend, William Molyneux, Locke did not, as far as the records go, actually attempt to use the 'mathematical method' to apply logic to moral concepts. Instead he even modified his position slightly. In a letter to Molyneux he wrote repeating his claim, 'morality might be demonstrably made out', but demurred at the idea he was necessarily the one to carry it out!

During this conversation Locke comes to acknowledge the difficulties of using logical proofs in the field of morality, but then turns to his real concerns. In what ways can words used in moral judgements be made less uncertain, less vague, less ambivalent.

Moore: Today I want to talk about your boldest, rashest, most foolhardy claim.

Locke: That sounds ominous. What do you believe it was?

Moore: Your claim that morality was as capable of demonstration as mathematics.

Locke: I did say that, didn't I?

Moore: You did. Not once but several times.

Locke: Really?

Moore: Yes, really. Do you remember, 'moral Knowledge is as capable of real Certainty as Mathematicks' and 'Morality among the Sciences capable of Demonstration ... (its) Propositions as certain as any Demonstration in Euclid'?

Locke: I did say all that, I confess.

Moore: You even rated studying morality higher than all the other enquiries going on around you into the natural world, like those of your friend Boyle, claiming that 'Morality is the proper Science and Business of Mankind in General'.

Locke: I said that because its enquiry concerns how we should live.

Moore: That makes it important, yes, but you didn't argue, let alone prove, morality was amenable to logical proof.

Locke: I did try to put together an argument. Friends pressed me.

Moore: One close friend in particular. I understand William Molyneux was very keen.

Locke: William begged me to write a treatise of morals. He continued to urge me to do it when he came to stay at Oates, where I was living with the Mashams after returning from Holland. I did warn him I wasn't sure whether I could do it.

Moore: If it were a treatise on morals we were talking about, of course you could produce one. But not a Q.E.D. No one could. I don't believe it can be done. Not only is morality not capable of mathematical demonstration, I'm going to try to convince you – to use your own expression – there can be no 'algebra' of morality.

Locke: So I was right to give up.

Moore: No, not at all. What I hope to do is show you there are steps we can take towards finding ways to reach some sort of agreement on what can be usefully said concerning key words in moral judgements.

Locke: You're setting yourself a tough task.

Moore: But a necessary one. After all, where you and I are in perfect agreement is on the importance of understanding the significance for our lives of the words we use when making moral judgements.

Locke: That only makes it an even tougher task!

Moore: Not really. Because what I'm planning is to use your own insights into the nature of words and meanings. You, not me, will be doing the work.

Locke: This might be interesting.

Moore: Do you recall your comments on moral words such as 'justice'?

Locke: Remind me.

Moore: If you want to check, it was in Book III in *An Essay Concerning Human Understanding*, Chapter 1X, entitled 'Of the Imperfection of Words'. You wrote:

> ... moral Words have seldom, in two different Men, the same precise signification. … since one Man's Complex Idea seldom agrees with another, and often differs from his own, from that which he had yesterday, or will have to-morrow.

Locke: Yes, that's what I believe. The meaning of such words is necessarily uncertain, vague, ambivalent.

Moore: There lies the seeds of misunderstanding. Unlike the certainty and precision of numbers: 2 + 2 x 5 has got to equal 20 precisely, definitively. And yet the fact that words excite meanings that are uncertain, vague, ambivalent is a consequence, as we have already seen, of the way language works. You were the one who persuaded me that the meanings of words are in the last resort located in our own minds. Remember: 'Words in their primary or immediate Signification, stand for nothing, but the Ideas in the Mind of him that uses them'.

Locke: What else could they stand for?

Moore: Precisely. And you go on: 'it is a perverting of the use of Words, and brings unavoidable Obscurity and Confusion into their Signification, whenever we make them stand for anything, but those Ideas we have in our own Minds.'

Locke: I do believe the mind is the great creator of meanings for each individual. Each mind takes the words it hears and annexes them to its ideas of the world. Meanings emerge from the complex filtering processes by which each individual mind fuses public words with their private ideas.

Moore: So we agree meanings are mind-dependent. Each mind making meanings for itself.

Locke: It's not the whole story, but mind-dependent will do for the moment. But don't overlook the ways we are all tacitly engaged in secretly referring.

Moore: I know. 'Secret Reference', the tacit assumption we make that the meanings words have for us are the meanings others have in their minds. A useful working hypothesis but not true of course. Sometimes our meanings are the same as those of other people, sometimes they're not.

Locke: Exactly. But you can see why I believe our use of language begins and ends in imprecision, though, fortunately, the degree of imprecision can vary!

Moore: It can indeed. You are returning once again to a fundamental point of yours: the meanings of the words we use are inherently indeterminate. That's how I came to see that morality cannot be demonstrable in the way mathematics is. I simply followed through on your insights into the nature of meaning, in particular how each individual can't help but have a highly personal relation with public words and private meanings.

Locke: I accept I may have overstated my point on morality. But it seems you're missing something that's truly important to me. When I claimed morality was demonstrable it was because I wanted it to be! Wishful thinking you may say, but I believe we need a foundation for our moral language. I wanted to be able to establish some way of gaining a degree of certainty of meaning for words like 'justice'. Yet at the same time I knew full well, and said repeatedly that words have naturally no signification. Clearly it was going to be extremely difficult to reach agreement.

Moore: Very difficult, precisely because of your radical view of meaning. As you put it in your favoured simile, words are like knots tying the bundle of ideas the mind collects. Sometimes, for some words, the knotted bundle one mind has collected is reasonably similar to the collection another mind has made. But it's rare, perhaps impossible, because of our different experiences of life, for two collections tied by the same knot to be identical.

Locke: I know. Nevertheless what I was looking for was some way to get closer to a generally accepted meaning for moral terms such as 'justice', however difficult. You did read the chapter in the *Essay* on 'Abuse of Words'?

Moore: Of course. And the one on 'Imperfections of Words' and 'Remedies for the Imperfections and Abuses of Words'. Yes, I read them all several times!

Locke: And so, rightly, I persuaded you there could not be an algebra of ethics.

Moore: You persuaded me precisely because of your repeated insistence that the use of language is both fundamentally and irrevocably subjective. Subjectivity is the cross you have all us language users bear. It's a heavy cross. And it's this innate subjectivity that will not allow moral codes to be as demonstrable in a strong sense as mathematics.

Locke: I must admit, looking at my arguments again, I agree with you. I'm afraid my arguments persuade me too. I could never demonstrate morality was amenable to logical proof. More's the pity.

Moore: Don't despair. From elsewhere in your own work I believe we can find two grounds for a degree of optimism. The first concerns words and their meanings. Let's work an example to pin the problem down. Take the ideas the word 'torture' excites in moral judgements such as: 'it is morally wrong to inflict gratuitous pain', or just 'torture is wrong'. For me the word 'torture' excites ideas about inflicting pain, either as a punishment or for the purpose of extorting a confession or information from an accused person.

Locke: Those ideas are certainly part of the bundle the word 'torture' ties for me. There's also the question for me of the value of what is gained by torturing an individual. It might for example yield knowledge leading to the saving of many lives. The pain inflicted might not be gratuitous.

Moore: You see, we're already getting somewhere. We're beginning to unravel some of the strands of meaning the word knots for each of us. In Chapter 1X you despaired, reminding us, 'these moral words are, in most Men's mouths, little more than bare Sounds, when they have any [signification] 'tis for the most part but very loose and undetermined, and consequently obscure and confused'. Yet here we are, you and I, learning about our individual bundles tied by the word 'torture'. So far the 'value' of what is learnt by torturing had not figured in mine.

Locke: Whereas for me that strand is crucial. You're making me see, I suppose, that if we hadn't discussed our individual strands, we'd never have unearthed this particular difference.

Moore: That's right. Let's push the example a bit further. Suppose I put the word whose meaning we have been exploring into a moral judgement and claim: 'Waterboarding is torture'. Following your account, though you and I might come to agree on the meaning for us of this moral judgement because we can discuss our individual bundles, I'm pretty sure we would not win universal consent. For some 'waterboarding' may fall within their ideas of what constitutes 'torture', for others it may not.

Locke: What's 'waterboarding'?

Moore: There are at least two ways of looking at the ideas the word excites. One tries to avoid a moral judgement, the other's morally loaded. The first might run: 'Waterboarding is a form of interrogation of a prisoner to elicit information.

It consists of first strapping down a prisoner supine on a board, covering his mouth with a cloth, and then pouring water over his face in a continuous stream. Among other effects, it causes fear of drowning, asphyxiation, rapid heartbeats ...' I could go on.

Locke: No, no, you've made your point. The interrogators I suppose believe the prisoner, after such treatment, will yield up valuable information. Hmm! What's the second account?

Moore: It might run: 'Waterboarding is a form of torture used in interrogating prisoners. It induces terrifying fear of death by drowning. In contrast to submerging the head face downwards in water, waterboarding precipitates an almost immediate gag reflex, causing extreme pain, damage to the lungs, brain damage from oxygen deprivation, lasting psychological damage and, if uninterrupted, death ...'

Locke: Enough of that. Yours I've learnt is a lawful country. Don't you have laws against practices like waterboarding?

Moore: The UK has certainly signed up to an International Convention Against Torture. All signatories have agreed they are subject to the explicit prohibition of torture under any conditions. And that's not all. We are also signatories to the *Universal Declaration of Human Rights*. Its 'Article Five' states, 'No one shall be subjected to torture, or to cruel, inhuman or degrading treatment or punishment.'

Locke: So there are now international laws against torture. But we come back to language. Laws are written in words. And words always require some interpreting, some unravelling of the ideas they excite. No wonder lawyers are kept busy!

Moore: We are back to words knotting bundles. Exactly as you would predict, there are broader and narrower construals of 'torture'. In some construals waterboarding is not classed as torture. As you would also expect, given what you wrote about individuals changing their minds about the meanings of moral words, you won't be surprised that signatories behave in the same way. Our own record, for instance, is not impeccable. We are not alone, of course, in shifting our moral position. Governments may declare at time-T waterboarding was legal, then at time-T+10 years declare it illegal.

Locke: Where's this argument taking us?

Moore: To my belief, or rather hope, that careful analysis of what we each have in mind by 'torture' might lead to an agreement about its meaning.

Locke: So you think that if more of us more often made a more careful analysis of such moral words as 'torture', there could eventually be an agreement on what I call a 'Common Acceptation' of its signification?

Moore: I'm hopeful.

Locke: I'm sceptical. From where do you draw hope?

Moore: Your insistence on the need for personal affirmation.

Locke: Personal affirmation! I'm sure I never used such a ponderous expression. What do you have in mind?

Moore: True, you didn't use that phrase, but it's from you I realised the importance for our use of language to, where it matters, personally affirm our beliefs. It's where I'm convinced we have to start.

Locke: Go on. What do we have to do?

Moore: Do you recall that in the bulk of Book III, 'Of Words or Language in General', you explore the problems of meanings that different categories of words excite. For example, words for simple ideas, 'hot', 'cold', 'sweet', 'bitter', 'hard' ... words for substances, like 'gold', words for abstract terms like 'torture'.

Locke: Of course. And don't forget particles. I was pleased with what I wrote about particles.

Moore: I won't forget them. But towards the end of Book III you change gear.

Locke: Do I?

Moore: Yes. You make a change I believe that has gone largely unnoticed. You shift from exploring the problems raised by the meanings of categories of words to considering the impact the subjectivity of meaning must have for the use of words in propositions.

Locke: For example?

Moore: Let's take your own your favoured example, 'Gold is malleable'. You say this then correct yourself. You remind us that we should never make statements that sound impersonal, objective. What we should say, you claim, is preface the proposition with a phrase acknowledging the limitations of our knowledge. In short we should say, 'What I call "gold" is malleable'.

Locke: Yes because that's as much as we really know, not knowing its essence.

Moore: What strikes me is that the phrase 'what I call' is a kind of speech act – it's personally affirming, making each individual take responsibility for the truth of a proposition. Without the phrase the proposition appears to affirm a truth: gold is malleable. With the phrase the proposition is placed, quite properly, within a personal view. That's what I have in mind when I talk about making a personal affirmation.

Locke: What's a speech act?

Moore: That's for another day. Speech acts come out of the work of an intriguing Oxford philosopher. Very briefly, when you say something, you do something, as when you promise something, or warn someone, or congratulate them. Have a look at J. L. Austin's *How to Do Things with Words*. It's on my shelves.

Locke: Sounds interesting.

Moore: Another day. What's important here is you make us see that by introducing a phrase like 'what I call' or 'in my view', we avoid making any objective claim. That's what I believe we should do for all moral statements.

Locke: Let me see if I've got this straight. Rather than say flatly, 'waterboarding is torture', you'd have us say, 'waterboarding is what I call torture'.

Moore: Exactly. That's what you'd have us say.

Locke: What makes you believe each of us personally affirming moral statements provides any grounds for a meeting of minds on what is to count as the meanings of moral terms?

Moore: Well, for a start, personally affirming invites the hearer to do exactly what we want them to do: ask why. Why do you call waterboarding 'torture'? This should lead to the kind of analysis we were talking about earlier. Some unpacking of the complex ideas the word 'torture' excites in our minds. Find out how far the bundle of ideas the word knots for each of us overlaps, or more likely perhaps, diverges.

Locke: You believe that particular process of analysis is what these international conventions should be subject to?

Moore: All sorts of controversial issues should be subject to it. We should own up to our personal responsibility for what we claim.

Locke: But why might that lead to any agreement on their meanings?

Moore: Not least because we share scruples. Pathological cases aside, I believe human beings share very similar moral scruples. Certain behaviours feel wrong. Cruelty, especially to people weaker than oneself, is wrong.

Locke: Don't certain behaviours also feel right? Acts of compassion, performing selfless acts, serving others all feel right. You believe these shared moral scruples provide the raw material out of which we might build a common moral code?

Moore: Cultures permitting, yes.

Locke: That sounds to me like an expression of faith in human beings.

Moore: Maybe you're right. That belief is part of my faith.

Locke: Not demonstrable then!

Moore: Not as demonstrable as mathematics. No algebra for ethics. But potential grounds for a meeting of minds?

Locke: Where human beings' goodwill is concerned, I suspect you're more of an optimist about people than I am. Maybe though William Molyneux was right. We should consider writing a treatise on morals. It could serve as a sequel to my last work, *The Conduct of the Understanding*.

Moore: I have sometimes thought that the 'Conduct' should have been Book V of *An Essay Concerning Human Understanding*.

Locke: Maybe. In the meantime I see I'm going to have to re-write my claims about morality.

Moore: Retracting your claims about demonstrability. Though I'm not sure I can get a treatise by you published!

Conversation Four

'Happiness ... everyone constantly pursues.'

Book II

An Essay Concerning Human Understanding

The Pursuit of Happiness: Locke and Moore at Odds

This conversation focuses on a disagreement between Locke and Moore on the nature of happiness. Locke sees happiness as a goal. He writes, 'the highest perfection of intellectual nature lies in a careful and constant pursuit of true and solid Happiness.' Moore disagrees. He believes happiness is epiphenomenal – a feeling that arises in association with some activity but is not the purpose of that activity. Happiness as Moore sees it cannot be pursued, only by chance experienced. Whose view will prevail? And has Locke overlooked his own second 'Secret Reference' by making happiness a thing to be pursued?

Moore: I've got a bone to pick with you.

Locke: Good. I like a nice meaty bone. What's its name?

Moore: Happiness. Specifically, how you define it and your view of what its role is in our lives.

Locke: Didn't I make that clear in Book II and parts of Book IV?

Moore: You may have believed you did. But I'm not convinced. You wrote, you may recall, 'Happiness, in its full extent, is the utmost pleasure we are capable of.' You also claimed we are moved to act by desire for our own happiness.

Locke: **(Turning the pages of the *Essay*.)** What I actually asked was, 'What is it moves desire?' I answered my own question, 'Happiness, and that alone.'

Moore: There's part of my bone. I believe you overestimate the role of happiness and underestimate the complexity and diversity of desires.

Locke: Anything else?

Moore: Actually there is. You wrote about happiness as if it were something that could be pursued.

Locke: **(Turning the pages.)** Strictly I wrote, 'The necessity of pursuing true Happiness [is] the Foundation of all Liberty.'

Moore: And capped it off claiming that 'the highest perfection of intellectual nature lies in a careful and constant pursuit of true and solid Happiness.' Have I cited you correctly?

Locke: **(Turning the pages.)** I must admit you have.

Moore: In that case everything you said about happiness is my bone.

Locke: But what exactly is your beef? I like your meaty idioms. We didn't have so many of those in my time.

Moore: Fundamentally I don't agree with the supreme role you assign to happiness as the mover and shaper of our lives.

Locke: You don't think happiness is important?

Moore: I didn't say that. But let's begin, where you taught me to begin, with the word itself, 'happiness'. Not its phonetics but its syntax. The word is a noun.

Locke: Obviously.

Moore: And people are inclined to believe nouns name things. We saw that when we were discussing your second 'Secret Reference'. People believe words 'stand for the reality of Things'.

Locke: Are you saying happiness doesn't exist?

Moore: No, I'm saying when you write that happiness, and happiness alone, is what moves us to act, readers in thrall to the second 'Secret Reference' might believe you conceive happiness to be a thing, an entity existing somewhere out there, that we, by diligently searching, by earnest pursuit, might one day find.

Locke: I didn't put it like that.

Moore: Maybe not. But if you think back to our conversation on your second 'Secret Reference', you can see how easy it would be for people to see 'happiness' as standing for a real thing in the world.

Locke: Let's take a step back. What have you got against the idea that we pursue happiness?

Moore: Well, to start with, whatever your readers may think surely you don't believe happiness is a thing. You who taught us in Book III of the *Essay* that the meaning of abstract words, General Terms you called them, is, I quote you, 'nothing but a relation that by the Mind of Man, is added to them.'

Locke: I did say that. It's what I believe is the case for the meaning of general terms.

Moore: So you're not saying there's some abstract stuff out there called 'happiness', but rather that the mind of man creates the idea of happiness.

Locke: Which man then pursues.

Moore: But what exactly does he pursue? I don't suppose you've had a chance to read Whitehead.

Locke: Whitehead? Who's Whitehead?

Moore: Mathematician, Philosopher, Fellow of Trinity College, Cambridge, last century. He wrote, and this should interest you, 'Language foists on us exact concepts as though they represented the immediate deliverance of experience.' In our conversation on your second 'Secret Reference' we ruled out any possibility of foisting of that sort. It was from you I learnt that's exactly what words don't do, they don't express the immediate delivery of experience. The individual mind has always got to play its part.

Locke: You're right of course. I think I'd better read some Whitehead. I guess his book is somewhere on your shelves.

Moore: It should be, unless someone has failed to return it. The title is: *The Organisation of Thought*. So can we agree the meaning of happiness is not out there in the world, but up here, in the mind, subjective, private, provisional, uncertain?

Locke: We can. But your insistence that happiness is not something to be pursued is intriguing me. Tell me, what ideas does the word 'happiness' excite in your mind? What does the workmanship of your mind produce for you?

Moore: I use the word to characterise a transient state that may unexpectedly overtake some individuals living in a certain kind of way. It's, as I see it, a by-product of something else, it's derivative, secondary, not primal.

Locke: So you believe happiness is epiphenomenal.

Moore: 'Epiphenomenal' is one of those words like 'rebarbative' or 'teleological', whose meaning I find difficult to pin down. I'm never quite sure what ideas they excite in my mind.

Locke: The ideas 'epiphenomenal' excite in my mind characterise something occurring as a result of something else – the way ripples disturb the surface of a pond after a stone's dropped. Or the patterns an ebbing sea leaves on a sandy beach.

Moore: Then 'epiphenomenal' is the right word. We shouldn't think of happiness as an entity in its own right, but as a consequence, a derivative. It's not something you can readily aim for, pursue or teach. Being happy happens, if it does, more or less by accident, when you're fully engaged in some other activity.

Locke: That's not the way I've been looking at it. Let me try a teleological argument on you.

Moore: Ah, 'teleological'! The ideas the word excites in my mind revolve around a belief that things, events, were planned to fulfil a purpose.

Locke: That's similar enough to what I have in mind.

Moore: Does this mean you still want to defend the view that happiness fulfils a purpose? The way you expressed it in the *Essay* was just to say that '... the highest perfection of intellectual nature lies in a careful and constant pursuit of true and solid Happiness.'

Locke: It may be that the word 'happiness' excites very different ideas in each of us. Let's see if that's the case. What I think we should do is explore the ideas the word 'happiness' excites. For me when I indulge in some activity, perhaps attempting to solve a problem, or, as I tried to do in the *Essay*, understand 'understanding', for me, in my bundle of ideas, we do so in pursuit of happiness.

Moore: And yes, it's an argument. We choose to do what we do in order to achieve happiness. The difficulty for me is I'm not sure that's where the route to happiness lies. If we set out with happiness as our goal, my experience is we don't achieve it. Happiness is more likely to steal up on us unsolicited. I'm persuaded there's something deeply epiphenomenal, to use your term, about happiness.

Locke: I never thought about it like that. You are being persuasive. I recall, for example, being overtaken by happiness at times on the rare occasions I was with William.

Moore: William?

Locke: William Molyneux, my Irish friend. And you?

Moore: Happiness, unsolicited, can steal up when I'm walking a ridge in the Scottish Highlands, or maybe I write a sonnet that isn't too bad, or our conversations go well.

Locke: A sonnet? Ah yes. I've been reading some of your poems in your collection *Voices in my Head*. I found it on your shelves.

Moore: I'm glad. Were there any you particularly liked?

Locke: I was struck by your sonnet entitled 'Rest'.

Moore: A poem very much of our times – and related to happiness.

Locke: Perhaps I should re-write those passages on happiness a little, emphasising its epiphenomenal nature.

Moore: Quite severely re-write I think! There's also the question of the complexity of human desires. You singled out happiness as the unique desire.

Locke: (**Turning the pages.**) Strictly what I wrote was, 'What is it moves desire? Happiness, and that alone.'

Moore: It's the 'alone' I'm querying.

Locke: You're saying there are other desires that move us equally.

Moore: A whole raft of them. Some are 'for', some are 'to'. The desire for physical gratifications of all sorts, for excellence, for reputation, for success, those desires all move us to act. The desire to avoid pain, boredom, to escape surroundings, to fulfil obligations, to avoid stern duty's pointing finger. Then there's compassion. It may be a far greater mover than happiness. When I see you suffer, I may suffer. That moves me to act to allay your suffering, so incidentally, epiphenomenally, allaying my suffering …

Locke: Yes, yes. I take your point. To be happy is one among a host of desires moving us to act, including compassion. I suspect when I was writing about happiness I may have confused 'pleasure' and 'happiness'.

Moore: You certainly appeared at one point to make 'pleasure' and 'pain' the foundation of your moral theory. In our last conversation we agreed that morality wasn't capable of demonstration. Perhaps feelings like 'happiness' are also more of an enigma than you originally thought.

Locke: **(Coughing hard.)** I have the feeling that I need to remember exactly what I wrote about general terms and read your friend Whitehead.

Moore: We can all be forgetful. I'll look forward to your reappraisal of the 'pursuit of happiness.' While you're at it, a similar problem arises with the 'pursuit of truth.' And you do tell us how much you relish truth!

Locke: I most certainly do.

Conversation Five

An Untenable Dualism

In this conversation Moore seeks Locke's support for a campaign he's privately pressing against the commonplace, frequently-cited distinction between the words 'objective' and 'subjective.' Putting it crudely, the objective is generally reckoned to be good, the subjective not so good. Science is taken as the model of an objective account of the world as we experience it; the humanities are believed to offer a subjective account of that world. Moore looks to Locke and his concept 'Secret Reference' to help him establish Moore's thesis: the objective has no true existence. As human beings we can only be more or less subjective. Moore is looking for grounds in the use of language to replace the dualism with a spectrum of subjectivity. Moore's spectrum has at one end: more dispassionate, at the other, less dispassionate. 'More dispassionate' approaches, but never reaches, objectivity. 'Less dispassionate' at its worst descends into fanaticism. Locke agrees, with some reservations about hyphenation, to help Moore.

Moore: I need your help.

Locke: What's the problem?

Moore: It's about a dualism, an either/or, one of many that are rife in the twenty-first century. I don't think it would be an exaggeration to say it's an intrinsic element of the intellectual climate of our age. So much so it goes unnoticed, worse, unquestioned.

Locke: I'm intrigued. Tell me about this dichotomy of yours.

Moore: It's the distinction between objective and subjective accounts of our experience of the world and our behaviour in it. Crudely put, objectivity is good, subjectivity, bad. But I believe the dualism is untenable.

Locke: And where do you think this dichotomy shows up most?

Moore: These binary oppositions are everywhere. Good/bad, left/right, true/false, right/wrong. They appear in the press, the media, the language of politicians, the general public, but especially scientists, natural and social.

Locke: Scientists – now there's a class of person that's come into being in your modern times. But why them especially?

Moore: Nearly every discussion of the importance of science nowadays assumes that science is sharply distinguished from the rest of our culture.

Locke: How do they say it's distinguished?

Moore: By its methods – formulating and testing hypotheses by linking systematic observations of the natural world with controlled experiments. Basically the tacit assumption is the results achieved are 'objective'. Other pursuits of knowledge are 'subjective'.

Locke: If I'm going to help you, you need to help me. Tell me - what do you understand by the words 'objective' and 'subjective'? What ideas do they excite in your mind?

Moore: A number of things. Essentially I suppose those who seek 'objectivity' seek to eliminate from scientific enquiry the human element, the personal. It's part of the goal to make scientific judgements appear value-free.

Locke: And 'subjectivity'?

Moore: Being 'subjective' for me is accepting the importance of the personal, of feelings, opinions, reactions. Think of wine. The judgements of connoisseurs, for example, are personal. You might not think so but even mathematicians can be connoisseurs, can be personal. Connoisseurs of the elegance of simplicity may prefer one proof rather than another because it appears simpler.

Locke: And you're convinced this dichotomy is false?

Moore: Absolutely. The reason I need your help is that I believe that in *An Essay Concerning Human Understanding* there's a grenade that, properly primed, would explode the distinction, show it to be fundamentally wrong.

Locke: Are you talking about my ideas on 'Secret Reference'? My account of the underpinnings of language understanding?

Moore: Yes. 'Secret Reference'. I need to continue to explore it in greater detail with you. One of its consequences you spell out at some length is the necessarily provisional and uncertain nature of our understanding of each other's language. Can we push that further?

Locke: Push away.

Moore: Using your idea of 'Secret Reference' I think we can demonstrate that the process of scientific enquiry also has, ultimately, an ineluctable subjective trace. In short, I believe you can free us from the shackles of 'objectivity', demonstrate once and for all that the disjunction between objective and subjective accounts of our knowledge of the world is an untenable dualism.

Locke: I'd welcome the chance to demonstrate something successfully, since I failed so miserably with morality!

Moore: There's nothing wrong with being wrong. So long as you recognise the wrongdoing!

Locke: I may be able to help, but first I have a question for you. What lies behind this 21st century commitment to objectivity?

Moore: I'm not enough of a historian of science to answer that, I'm afraid. I can only speculate.

Locke: Speculate away!

Moore: Well, an obvious place to begin might be the dawn of the Age of Reason, generally known as the Enlightenment.

Locke: Yes I've heard that expression.

Moore: A convenient date might be the founding of the Royal Society, in your prime time! Robert Boyle and Isaac Newton of course were early members.

Locke: I was a Fellow too you know! The Royal Society's full title might help your search for the origins of a commitment to objectivity. We knew it as The Royal Society for the Improving of Natural Knowledge.

Moore: 'Improving' is not claiming 'objectivity'.

Locke: True. Our motto, as you know, expressed our aim, 'Nullius in Verba'. Remind me. How good is your Latin?

Moore: In my day passing a Latin exam was a prerequisite for entering Cambridge. Fortunately I passed! 'Nullius in Verba'? I believe 'Take nobody's word for it' is the rough paraphrase the Royal Society adopts.

Locke: As a rough paraphrase it will do. What we aimed to do was rely on observation, conjecture, experiment, testing – not on statements by authorities.

Moore: Wasn't Boyle a friend?

Locke: More than a friend, Robert was my scientific mentor.

Moore: Didn't he ask you to carry out some research on the minerals in the Somerset mines and keep a record of changes in the temperature?

Locke: He did and I did. But it wasn't a success. The miners wouldn't let me join them. I fear I wasn't cut out for that sort of research. With Isaac, however, it was a different story. We corresponded not about his optics, his mathematics, but about our different interpretation of the letters of

St Paul. You have to recall in those days we had two books to read, the Bible and the Book of Nature.

Moore: Actually I think I should go back a bit earlier in time to find when the seeds of the Age of Reason were sown.

Locke: Back to when?

Moore: Back to Copernicus.

Locke: Copernicus! Nicolaus Copernicus, the Polish astronomer. If my memory serves me right, wasn't he round about the mid-fifteenth to the mid-sixteenth century? That's quite a bit earlier. But why Copernicus?

Moore: Well it was Copernicus who was prepared to abandon the immediate evidence of the senses, the ultimate subjective experience, in favour, or so it appeared, of exalting the mind, reason, the objective perspective.

Locke: I hadn't quite seen it like that.

Moore: In his book, *De revolutionibus orbium coelestium*, completed 1530, he rejected the evidence of the senses, which presents us with the apparently irresistible evidence of the sun rising daily in the east, travelling across the sky to set in the west. Instead of taking the earth to be the centre of the universe, he made the sun its centre. With one leap he replaced a geocentric stance with a heliocentric model of the solar system.

Locke: True, but what follows?

Moore: To all and sundry, but especially the Catholic Church, this was obviously nonsense. Our language tells us quite clearly, 'the sun rises' and 'the sun sets.' The evidence of our eyes is, they thought, irresistible. For them Ptolemy was right.

Locke: Claudius Ptolemy, second-century, eminent astronomer. Now we're going back even earlier!

Moore: True, but in his book, *Almagest*, he declared the sun, the stars, the planets revolve around the earth.

Locke: You must admit that to an earthbound observer it does look like that. The Earth does not seem to move, does it? Appears in fact completely at rest. You can see why it was generally concluded that the Earth is the centre of the universe.

Moore: Yes. Easy to see why in spite of the shortcomings of the geocentric view as a description of the universe.

Locke: Presumably though the Church would have nodded comfortably. Why else would God have created the universe?

Moore: The fact is that while Copernicus' model of a sun-centred solar system undoubtedly simplified Ptolemy's complex model, it too was wrong. Though not for the reasons the Church and others rejected his view. It was not until Kepler's laws of planetary motion proposed elliptical, not Copernicus' circular, orbits for the movements of the planets that the heliocentric system won general acceptance.

Locke: Granted all that. But how does this make Copernicus a possible father of your position on the untenability of the objective/subjective dualism?

Moore: Well, I'm only speculating but it seems to me what Copernicus did in effect was to abandon relying on the evidence of immediate experience to explain the solar system. Instead he advanced his heliocentric theory based on reason.

Locke: So he abandoned the anthropomorphism of the senses for the anthropomorphism of our reasoning.

Moore: If by that you mean man's perspective shifted from relying upon the data supplied by the senses to listening to the voice of reason, then yes. But in apparently exalting reason, in essence appearing to offer an 'objective account' of the universe, something important got left out and, alas, never put back.

Locke: What?

Moore: Imagination. To create a heliocentric model of the solar system Copernicus had to imagine a state of affairs that was believed not to exist. Creative acts of the imagination, backed by a reasoning mind, can change our understanding of the world. And that's what Copernicus did! Combined reason and imagination.

Locke: And you're going to tell me that acts of the imagination are essentially subjective, personal acts. Acts that may or may not be supported by reason.

Moore: Exactly. What is first imagined must then be by reason tested. Therefore, as I see it, there is no absolute disjunction between the subjective and the objective. The so-called 'objective' is rooted in the subjective. However what most certainly do exist are degrees of subjectivity. And that's where I particularly need your help.

Locke: Of course. As you suggest the key might lie in my account of 'Secret Reference'.

Moore: Exactly. We discussed 'Secret Reference' in some detail in our very first conversation. What was it we agreed?

Locke: Let me re-cap briefly. I reminded you that the first 'Secret Reference' served as my solution to a problem I saw as underlying our use of language.

Moore: Yes I remember the problem.

Locke: Alright. You tell me.

Moore: In Book III of the *Essay* you had insisted on a radical and apparently weird view of meaning. You claimed words had no meaning.

Locke: Not quite. I actually said words have no meaning until …

Moore: Until?

Locke: Words have no meaning, until each of us independently creates a meaning for ourselves by filtering public words through private processes in our own minds.

Moore: Those weren't your exact words, were they? But what is crucial is your conclusion: meanings in the last resort are mind-dependent, personal, subjective.

Locke: Right. What's wrong is that by and large individuals don't recognise that they are the ones who create meanings for themselves. Without acknowledging it they act as if the words they use have the same meaning for others as they do for them.

Moore: It's this 'acting as if' you call 'Secret Reference'.

Locke: You, I recall, like to call it 'tacit supposing'.

Moore: Yes, and like you, I think tacitly supposing my words are exciting the same meaning in your head as they do in mine is a reasonable working hypothesis. It's a place to start.

Locke: But no more than that. It's a plausible working hypothesis but false, as we regularly discover when we find ourselves misunderstanding each other, the ideas excited by our words diverging from those of the person we're talking to. We seem surprised, even put out that the other hasn't understood! Acknowledging 'Secret Reference' is certainly a necessary step towards avoiding misunderstanding each other, but it's not in itself sufficient. There's another factor I don't think we mentioned earlier, time.

Moore: Time? What do you mean?

Locke: As well as acknowledging 'Secret Reference' it can help us communicate effectively if we've known our interlocutor for some time. I recall my great friend William Molyneux saying to me once when he was staying over at Oates, "I think I'm getting to know you well enough to begin to understand what you're talking about." Very perceptive, William. He saw that the better we know people, the more intimate our conversation, the closer our private meanings may become. But I think it's not the first 'Secret Reference' that bears on your untenable dualism as much as the second.

Moore: Your second 'Secret Reference' claims that in using language we take for granted words stand for things in the world.

Locke: Or to use your language, we tacitly suppose words, as I said 'stand for the reality of Things'.

Moore: And as I recall you immediately chide us for forgetting what words really stand for.

Locke: I have it here, Book III, Chapter II, 'it is a perverting the use of words and brings unavoidable Obscurity and Confusion into their Signification, whenever we make them stand for anything, but those Ideas we have in our own Minds.' What does that say for the possibility of being 'objective'?

Moore: It says that being objective is ultimately impossible. Your second 'Secret Reference' helps us recognise that though we may step back from some aspects of ourselves, certain feelings, prejudices, ingrained reactions, we can never step wholly outside ourselves in seeking to understand the world. In short we're all ultimately victims of our own tacit supposings.

Locke: Particularly since 'secretly referring', or 'tacitly supposing', have to be personal acts, ineluctably subjective.

Moore: So we're agreed, the dualism is untenable. Even for practising scientists, the best of whom may try their hardest not to be influenced by their preconceptions, feelings, wishes, hopes.

Locke: In its absolute form the dualism, as you call it, is untenable, yes. But it's not as simple as that. As you said earlier, there are degrees of subjectivity.

Moore: True. What I think we should be trying to do is replace the dualism by a spectrum of subjectivity. At one end of the subjectivity spectrum is 'more dispassionate', at the other end, 'less dispassionate'. Whilst no statement is totally objective, no utterer totally dispassionate, statements can be more or less subjective, utterers more or less dispassionate. Perhaps 'more or less' is the expression I want to replace 'either/or'.

Locke: That sounds a better way of looking at it. Certainly for moral issues, social issues, aesthetic judgements, I agree with your wanting to replace a black/white dichotomy with a spectrum or gradient of some kind, measuring degrees of subjectivity, degrees of personal feeling. Most interesting. Have you an example we could look at?

Moore: Well, there's an important proposition bedevilling the 21st century. So important it arouses strong feelings for and against. If we look at the language these views are expressed in, we might get pointers to a possible direction in which to look.

Locke: What's the statement?

Moore: 'Global warming is man-made.'

Locke: That's at least two problems of understanding. First, what do individuals believe counts as – what did you call it – *global warming*?

Moore: *Global warming*, people believe with varying degrees of understanding, refers to the global average-temperature increase that has been observed over the last hundred years or more. Because temperatures are measurable and comparable with temperatures of other times, there's pretty much agreement that our earth is warming. The controversy comes with the judgement.

Locke: I know a little about temperature. It was the temperature in the Somerset mines Robert Boyle wanted me to measure. Is the judgement your scientists are making that this rise in temperature is due to human influence?

Moore: The majority, yes. More specifically, the claim is that the increase is caused by growing concentrations of what we call greenhouse gases resulting from human activities such as the burning of fossil fuels, rapid deforestation, polluting the oceans. In brief, global warming in the judgement of many is man-made. Others disagree.

Locke: So we should look at the language in which each contesting faction expresses its view.

Moore: There's an awful lot been said and written. I'll take just two examples. The first seems to me less subjective, more dispassionate. Some, in old language, might even be tempted to call it 'objective'. The other strikes me as clearly more subjective, less dispassionate. The first is from a scientist, a Professor of Mathematical Astrophysics at Cambridge University, Nigel Weiss. He affirms the pronouncements of the Intergovernmental Panel on Climate Change, the IPCC. The IPCC's findings stress the view that humans are the most likely cause of global warming. In his support Weiss countered the sceptics' view that sunspot activity is a more significant cause of climate change than human influence. He wrote: 'Although solar activity has an effect on the climate, these changes are small compared with those associated with global warming.' He added: 'Any global cooling associated with a fall in solar activity would not significantly affect the global warming caused by greenhouse gases.'

Locke: The language strikes me as measured, offers testable claims, challengeable for truth. One could, for example, look at whether other astrophysicists agree with his account of the effects of sunspot activity. What's the other example?

Moore: It's from a documentary on a television channel called, *The Great Global Warming Swindle*. In it man-made climate change is called 'a lie … the biggest scam of modern times.' It continues,

> The truth is that global warming is a multibillion dollar worldwide industry: supported by scientists peddling scare stories to chase funding,

and propped up by complicit politicians and the media, … solar activity is far more likely to be the culprit.

Locke: That language would certainly register on my scale as more subjective, less dispassionate. The use of words like 'swindle', 'lie', 'scam', 'fanatically', 'peddling', 'propped up', all seemed aimed to inflame the passions, subdue the impulse to reflect, to analyse and to consider dispassionately the evidence for believing global warming is man-made.

Moore: To appeal to the emotional rather than the cognitive level.

Locke: If that's how you put it these days. The different assessments on sunspot activity would need following up.

Moore: I could of course have reversed the examples. Found measured language for the second position, inflaming language for the first. The point was not the truth of the positions, but to demonstrate the character of the language.

Locke: If we're looking at 'more or less' the language of your professor is clearly more dispassionate than the language of your television documentary.

Moore: But still not objective.

Locke: No, not objective. In the last resort astronomer Weiss' own tacit supposings must colour his view of the material world. And these personal views must underlie his language, influencing the ideas his words excite for him. It cannot be otherwise.

Moore: We do agree then. However far in our judgements we are able to step back from our immediate feelings, we can never step entirely outside ourselves. Your second secret reference, our tacitly supposing words stand for 'the reality of Things', has undoubtedly helped to demonstrate the dualism is untenable. If words cannot in the last resort stand for anything other than ideas in our minds, then a personal element must always remain with us. In the case of Copernicus, the personal element was imagination. Nothing else is possible.

Locke: Let's think instead then about your suggestion of a spectrum of subjectivity.

Moore: A rating perhaps from low subjectivity at the more dispassionate end to high subjectivity at the less dispassionate end, depending upon the language, the words, the phrases being used. The lower the level of subjectivity the higher the confidence in the user and their language.

Locke: You could put it that way. Frequency of certain types of expression in an argument could also be a significant marker.

Moore: At the very least a spectrum of subjectivity wouldn't countenance pure objectivity. We might furthermore find some help in the research computational linguists are currently doing.

Locke: Computational linguists?

Moore: Yes, language experts using computers to do textual analysis to try and identify and extract information about the feelings and attitudes of the writer of a text. In short, their degree of subjectivity.

Locke: You really do live in a different world! But you're right, acknowledging a spectrum of subjectivity should put us in a better position to assess the believability of a judgement. It could help us understand why we might be inclined to accept as true what certain people say, and not others. But didn't you say there were other dualisms you distrusted?

Moore: Indeed there are – one I feel particularly strongly about is the generally held, false view of an opposition between the mind and the body. Here I think we can get some help not so much from words but from the hyphen. I want to praise the hyphen. Hyphenating matters!

Locke: What on earth are you talking about?

Moore: Well, mind-hyphen-body, 'mind-body' suggests to me that the mind and body are inextricably bound together. Not two separate entities disjoined, but forever conjoined.

Locke: Descartes wouldn't approve!

Moore: Descartes has cast a long shadow.

Locke: (**Hacking cough**.) Another evening, perhaps.

Moore: Agreed. Take care with that chest of yours!

CONVERSATION SIX

Locke's Parrot: What 'Puts a Perfect Distinction Between Man and Brutes?'

In this their sixth conversation John Locke and Terence Moore consider a question not fully answered even today: what might count as the key distinction between man and animals, or in Locke's phrase what 'puts a perfect distinction between Man and Brutes.'? In *An Essay Concerning Human Understanding* Locke considers two possible linguistic candidates: the ability to use language appropriately, and the ability to 'quit Particulars'. As Locke and Moore explore these possibilities they come to see that the distinction between man and animals is not as clear-cut as previous philosophers such as Descartes had believed. Locke tentatively posits a third possible distinction based on a central idea in his *Essay*, 'Secret Reference' – one Moore is compelled to dismiss, though he, in return, also tentatively, offers a fourth possible distinction.

Moore: I want to talk to you about your parrot.

Locke: My parrot! I don't have a parrot - never have had!

Moore: No, but you did talk about one, didn't you – in one of the chapters in *An Essay Concerning Human Understanding* – the one on identity and diversity.

Locke: Oh, you mean that old, grey Brazilian parrot. Did you know I added that chapter to the second edition of the *Essay*?

Moore: I did, but only because I've read what Lockeian scholars write. What made you add it?

Locke: Blame René!

Moore: René?

Locke: René Descartes. His *Meditations* had me brooding about personal identity – where does it lie? So I tried, not very successfully I admit, to disentangle my rambling speculations about the ways our memory and consciousness interact to create our idea of ourselves.

Moore: Actually it isn't problems of identity I want to talk about this evening, though I'd like to on another occasion. Can we start with your Brazilian parrot?

Locke: I can't imagine why.

Moore: In a nutshell because that Brazilian parrot supported an argument you were making about what, if anything, might count as the key distinction between man and animals. What, in your words, 'puts a perfect distinction between Man and Brutes.'

Locke: Oh yes, I remember. It was Descartes again that got me interested. He was convinced that humans were creatures of reason, animals were just machines, with no minds at all. Even those that uttered words such as magpies and parrots would, he believed, never respond appropriately. For him that was a perfect distinction. Well, I believed I had evidence of a parrot having just that capacity.

Moore: How exactly did the parrot help your case against Descartes?

Locke: Because it appeared perfectly able to use language to carry on a conversation in an appropriate manner.

Moore: You didn't observe the parrot yourself, though did you? Your conclusion wasn't the result of first-hand experience.

Locke: True. I took the story from Sir William Temple's memoirs. Sir William struck me as a reliable witness, and he'd heard the story at first-hand from Prince Maurice who was once the governor in Brazil.

Moore: So your evidence is third-hand! Still what *was* striking – as you described it – was the way the parrot actually handled the Prince's questions.

Locke: Exactly! That's what intrigued me. Descartes would never've credited it. A parrot carrying on a sensible conversation! Can I look at the exchange again? I've forgotten how it went.

Moore: Let me recap it for you. When the Prince asked the Parrot where was he from, the Parrot replied, 'From Marinnan.' The Prince followed this with the question, 'To whom do you belong?' to which the Parrot replied, 'A Portuguese.' Then the Prince asked what the Parrot did. The answer came back straightaway, 'I look after the chickens.' Apparently the Prince thought this funny, whereupon the Parrot, possibly a bit miffed, boasted, 'I do it very well.' And then demonstrated his method, by producing the clicks farmers make when attracting the attention of chickens.

Locke: You must admit the parrot's responses look pretty appropriate to the questions. As a linguist I'm sure you'd agree the parrot's replies show some syntactic sequencing, and a definite capacity to make judgements, and to recall absent actions.

Moore: True, but *only if* Sir William's account is reliable. The parrot might have been trained.

Locke: You're right, of course. My account is – how do you put it these days – anecdotal. But what intrigued me about that parrot was that though it had a bird body with a bird brain, that brain of his appeared to allow it to use language appropriately in a conversation.

Moore: So if, and it's a huge if, we were to believe Sir William's account, we could no longer believe, as Descartes did with absolute confidence, that using language appropriately served to put 'a perfect distinction between Man and Brutes.'

Locke: That was my point.

Moore: But your point successfully kills off any simple argument that using language appropriately serves as a key distinction between man and animals. It might all be down to training.

Locke: Alas, that too has to be true. Still I do have another linguistic feature I think that might serve as a 'perfect distinction'.

Moore: What's that?

Locke: Man's ability in using language to quit particulars. No animal I ever heard of was able to abstract from the specific circumstances of time and place to form a general concept.

Moore: Chomsky might well agree with you on this characteristic, though he uses a different vocabulary of course. As he puts it in *Cartesian Linguistics* the responses of animals are 'stimulus-bound', whereas for human beings responses can be 'stimulus-free' as well as 'stimulus-bound'.

Locke: *Cartesian Linguistics*. Hmm. Did he also write Lockeian Linguistics?

Moore: I'm afraid not. His subtitle for *Cartesian Linguistics* was *A Chapter in the History of Rationalist Thought*. Chomsky appears to have believed you, as an alleged empiricist, were outside the rationalist tradition.

Locke: You do know, don't you, that he was seriously mistaken! We must talk about that some more. What do you think Chomsky had in mind by 'stimulus-bound' and 'stimulus-free'?

Moore: Well, as an example, for an older generation the response to the greeting question, 'How do you do?' was formulaic, another question, 'How do you do?' A great deal of language is like that – formulaic, bound to a stimulus. Think of birthday greetings or farewells. Whereas responses to, for example, 'How are you?' are not tied to the stimulus. They can 'quit particulars', or be 'stimulus-free', and range unpredictably from 'Fine' to 'Don't ask?' to who knows what.

Locke: I see, though when I suggested that our ability to 'quit particulars' was a distinguishing mark, I was thinking more about our ability to abstract, to move away from the particular to form general ideas – ideas we then tied in our minds with words. From the experience of 'chalk', 'milk', 'snow', for example, we can abstract the idea of 'whiteness'. I knew of no evidence of animals having that capacity.

Moore: The drawback for your position is that the evidence is accumulating to show that quitting or not quitting particulars is unlikely to provide a perfect distinction either. The more we learn about animals, about birds, the less we can be sure about what they can and cannot do, including the range of their cognitive capacity to abstract and their ability to communicate with each other. In fact, once we acknowledge natural selection is not a creative force – it can only make use of the variations it's presented with – then it's plausible to suppose a species from which we humans may have evolved had similar, if less advanced, mental capabilities. Darwin certainly thought so.

Locke: Ah, Darwin, yes. I've dipped into his *Expression of the Emotions in Man and Animals*. You're right. He believed the mental capacities of man and animals differed only in degree. Do we have evidence of species having similar if less-advanced capabilities?

Moore: Quite a lot from monkeys of course but also from corvids. If you accept, which most of us do these days, that we have evolved from primates, then you could look at the behaviour of, for instance, macaque monkeys. Researchers on a Japanese island observed an inventive female macaque washing sand and grit off her sweet potatoes. You could argue she did this because she had formed some abstract notion, 'cleanliness'. It's reported some males caught onto the idea of 'cleanliness', though the older dominant ones never learnt the new behaviour. These monkeys may not be as smart as us but maybe it's a sliding scale: smart, smarter, smartest – monkeys, chimps and us.

Locke: You seem to be suggesting we shouldn't be looking for any perfect distinction at all.

Moore: I'm inclined more to a Darwinian spectrum of abilities.

Locke: A spectrum of abilities! There's a thought, though if we follow it through we shall have to change the preposition.

Moore: Change what preposition? Here we are into language, words and meanings again!

Locke: Of course. We've been looking at the question of 'What distinguishes man *from* animals?' But suppose it's the wrong question. Suppose the question we should be looking at is, 'What distinguishes man *amongst* animals?' 'From' begs the question, presupposes a distinction, and maybe points us in the wrong direction. But if we change 'from' to 'amongst' we are centred where we belong. Man is an animal. That, by the way, is the dividing line between me and Descartes. He believed, and I never did, that animals were essentially machines.

Moore: And a machine, he commented, 'never arranges words variously in response to the meaning of what is said in its presence.'

Locke: As my parrot did.

Moore: So you say! And of course if animals were seen as machines, Cartesians were free to treat animals inhumanly.

Locke: Could and did. But if we get the preposition right we can explore man's place amongst the animals, where we are on the spectrum. That would help resolve another problem for me with the way we've been putting the enquiry. Questions such as, 'What distinguishes man from animals?' always seems to me to be calling for one single, simple and final distinction – one true and only mark of man. One, incidentally, like rationality, that happens not only to extol the excellence of man over all other creatures, but also does wonders for man's self-esteem. Re-thinking in the light of our conversations so far, it could be the question has a complex of answers.

Moore: Part of which might be the mind's capacity to 'quit particulars.'

Locke: And part of which might be the ability to respond appropriately. Though neither of these provide *the* key distinction, both are probably there somewhere along the spectrum we're opening up. Rather than saying animals don't exercise these abilities, it'll probably turn out to be more accurate to say humans exercise them to a much greater degree than animals. Which sets me wondering about the far end of the spectrum, whether there's something we humans do in our use of language that animals definitely don't.

Moore: Back to the idea of a 'perfect distinction between Man and Brutes.'

Locke: Yes and no. Suppose we take my conjecture about the essential basis of language understanding? The conjecture I called 'Secret Reference'.

Moore: An idea that's been my guiding beacon ever since I realised its implications for our use of language. Your highly original response to the consequence of our primal linguistic condition – as you repeatedly made clear in the *Essay*, each of us humans, as far as the meaning of words is concerned, is locked in our own heads, a solitary, isolated state.

Locke: 'Words', I agree I might have said on more than one occasion …

Moore: Seven times in that short Chapter II, Book III!

Locke: Words 'in their primary or immediate Signification, stand for nothing, but the Ideas in the Mind of him that uses them'.

Moore: Which of course means that no one can ever know for certain what another person means by the words they use. It makes our understanding of others' meanings necessarily, not accidentally, provisional and uncertain. You manage to make meaning deeply paradoxical and inherently indeterminate.

Locke: That has to be true because as I certainly said, also on more than one occasion, the meanings of words are nothing but a relation that by the mind of Man is added to them. Meanings are the workmanship of the understanding.

Moore: And since the results of the workmanship of my mind are not identical with yours, I can't help but come up with my own meanings for words I hear you use – meanings that will to some extent, because our experience of the world has been different, diverge from yours. Your concept 'Secret Reference' helps to explain how we nevertheless do appear to communicate. Though our meanings are fundamentally private, you say we act as if they weren't. This tacit act of the imagination you make fundamental to our use of language. In essence your 'Secret Reference' serves as an essential working hypothesis for our sometimes more, sometimes less successful use of language.

Locke: True. If my conjecture is right, then the pertinent question for us here becomes: do animals 'secretly refer'? Though I have to admit I have no empirical evidence to show humans really do 'secretly refer' either.

Moore: I have good and bad news for you on that. The good news is that at least some evidence is accumulating that may possibly provide a physical basis in the brain for your conjecture that we 'secretly refer'.

Locke: Now that's exciting. Tell me about this new evidence.

Moore: Advances in neuroscience now make it possible to peer inside the brain. Researchers are finding a network of cells that fire in a creature's brain when it observes another creature performing an act it is able to perform, even though at that very moment it is not performing that action. In effect this network of cells in one brain reflects, or mirrors, an activity being performed by another individual. They're calling this network, 'mirror neurons'.

Locke: 'Mirror neurons'! How do they work exactly?

Moore: I'm taking the results of some experiments done in the University of Parma on the behaviour of monkeys. I think they were macaques. The researchers found that when one monkey, monkey A, reaches for a peanut certain neurons will fire. Much more interesting was the finding that these same neurons fired in another monkey, B, as he was watching monkey A reaching for the peanut.

Locke: So these monkeys appear to possess these mirror neurons you've been talking about. I need to read more about this research.

Moore: I'll give you some references later. What strikes me is that these mirror neurons could well provide the physical basis of your speculative 'Secret Reference', your working hypothesis underpinning our use of language. Suppose what's happening when we tacitly imagine others' words mean for them what they mean for us is that our mirror neurons are firing – B responding to A's public words but with the meanings those words excite in himself.

Locke: But B's neurons are not necessarily discharging to the same effect as A's. Not if his ideas excited by A's words are different. Similar perhaps but not a mirror. Can we really say mirror neurons are at work?

Moore: I'm only speculating it's true. But sometimes A and B's meanings probably are similar, sometimes possibly they are, sometimes not at all. There are times when we just don't understand what someone is saying or writing.

Locke: Absolutely. Sometimes we understand the words of others as they intend, sometimes we only think we do because of our tacit 'Secret Reference'. But is there any real evidence of these mirror neurons being involved in our understanding the language of others?

Moore: Some, a negative sort of evidence. Children with a dysfunctional mirror neuron network …

Locke: You mean children with broken mirrors?

Moore: Yes. Such children show the symptoms of those suffering from a condition we label 'autism'. Typically they avoid your gaze, appear unable to carry on an ordinary conversation, have difficulty understanding metaphors, seem oblivious of common social clues other children pick up naturally – in short they appear unable to mirror the brain activity of others.

Locke: I want to learn more about that research as well.

Moore: Of course. Though I should warn you the research is still in its early days. I'm leaping ahead a bit. But in time, the brain imaging techniques they're now using to establish the mirroring of activities in primates could be applied to see what's going on in our understanding of other people's use of language. Current work has been mainly on the mirror neuron systems in certain primates. That's the bad news by the way.

Locke: You mean that 'Secret Reference' may not be unique to humans?

Moore: If monkeys, however primitively, share our mirror-neuron network, 'Secret Reference' is not going to provide the 'perfect distinction' you were originally looking for – a cognitive capacity we have and animals definitely don't.

Locke: I think I'm about ready to give up on the idea of a perfect distinction. Mapping points on a spectrum of cognitive and affective abilities is, I suspect, likely to be the most fruitful way forward.

Moore: Yes, probably, but don't despair entirely of the idea of some kind of unique distinction. I have a small conjecture, but I'm afraid no hard evidence.

Locke: Really! Go on.

Moore: I suppose it's possible a significant distinction may lie in the way we use language. Animal languages, their systems of communication, appear to be shot through with what we would probably call imperatives and statements. Roughly, warning cries about dangers: 'Look out, there's an eagle/a leopard/ a snake!'; aggressive cries, 'Keep out!', 'Stay away!'; sexual cries, 'Come now, I'm ready!'; or statements of the sort a scout bee makes on returning to the hive, 'There's honey over there!', dancing the direction and the distance. What I find striking is what appears to be missing altogether.

Locke: What's missing?

Moore: Questions.

Locke: Interesting. You may be right. My Brazilian parrot wasn't reported to have asked questions.

Moore: We humans are constantly using language to ask questions. Physical questions, 'What is it?', 'How does it work?'; metaphysical questions, 'Why am I here?', 'Who am I?'

Locke: So we're back to questions of purpose and personal identity – the starting point you may recall of that Chapter I added to the *Essay*. You're suggesting there's no evidence of animal questioning, or doubting, no angst?

Moore: Not that I know of. The reason of course we continue to ask questions is that we continue to doubt the answers we're given. Maybe it's our use of language, allowing doubting, even scepticism, that might provide your 'perfect distinction'.

Locke: So that's Moore's conjecture. Humans can be sceptics. No bee, as far as we know, ever doubts the scout bee's dance indicating a source of honey.

Moore: There is one other human trait that just might provide your perfect distinction. I'm only speculating. I have no hard evidence.

Locke: Speculate away.

Moore: Humans laugh! Laughter might be the ultimate distinguishing mark. I've never heard of a scout bee sending the swarm off in the wrong direction. Then laughing his head off as he rests quietly in the hive!

Locke: He'd better not be there when they return! You've given me thoughts I need to mull over – after I've done some reading and catching up on this mirror-neuron research and bee behaviour.

Moore: I'll await the outcome of the mulling. Till next time then!

Conversation Seven

Orwell's Problem

In this conversation Locke and Moore discuss the power of the state and of the media to indoctrinate and possibly control people's ideas and beliefs by manipulating language. One particularly stark example of the exercise of that power is the fictional language 'Newspeak' created by George Orwell in his classic novel *1984*. In homage to Orwell, Chomsky called the problem of indoctrination through language, via spin, 'Orwell's Problem'.

The fundamental principles of Newspeak and its declared aim – to narrow the range of thought – challenge Locke's analysis of the workings of language. Locke, never a man to be found in 'a posture of blind credulity' – takes up the Newspeak challenge and pursues its implications for truth-telling.

Moore: Have you done your homework?

Locke: Read Orwell's *1984*? Of course. It was chilling – gave me goose pimples!

Moore: I'm not surprised.

Locke: I also did more than you asked. I went on to read an essay Orwell wrote before writing *1984*, his essay on *Politics and the English Language*. Because I knew of your interest in Noam Chomsky, I also added some political, not linguistic, Chomsky. I found his *Necessary Illusions: Thought Control in Democratic Societies* and *Manufacturing Consent* especially interesting.

Moore: Excellent. Orwell and Chomsky it seems to me shared one love and one hate. They each relish what they think of as the truth, while each detested the diet of lies, half, quarter, fractional truths they are fed by the people in power – in Chomsky's case corporate as well as state power.

Locke: Corporate power?

Moore: It's the name we give to the immense power of business, of large global corporations. A huge force to be reckoned with in our times.

Locke: I could never have imagined such a development.

Moore: Nor I at one time. But to go back to Orwell and Chomsky. Each hated and found morally revolting the hypocrisy of their rulers under the standard cover of what is commonly called 'realpolitik'.

Locke: 'Realpolitik'? That's a new word to me. What *ideas* does it excite in you?

Moore: Ideas about the use of power. Ensuring power is used after a realistic, but certainly not moral, assessment of what's good for one's own side and bad for one's enemies. The assessment is usually short-term and short-sighted. But tell me what particularly gave you goose pimples in *1984*?

Locke: The plight of Orwell's protagonist, of course. Winston Smith, the painful torture – the rat cage – and the degradation. They left Winston little more than a gin-sodden recluse, wasting away in the Chestnut Tree Café. But I was also especially struck by the fanatic Syme. I found him the most chilling individual.

Moore: The linguist Syme! One of the team creating the eleventh edition of the next Newspeak dictionary – the venomously orthodox, treacherous Syme.

Locke: You call him a linguist! Surely linguists love language. Syme was a hater of language! Do you recall the fanatical zeal he brought to the slaughter of words? Here let me read you a bit:

> We're destroying words, scores of them – we're cutting language to the bone. It's a beautiful thing, the destruction of words. … Don't you see the whole aim of Newspeak is to narrow the range of thought? In the end we shall make thoughtcrime literally impossible because there'll be no words in which to express it. The Revolution will be complete when the language is perfect.

Chilling, isn't it? Cutting the number of words is a plus for Syme precisely because he passionately believes it cuts the range of thought.

Moore: And that's exactly what I want to talk to you about – the relation between language and thought. Syme clearly takes a different view of words and meanings from yours.

Locke: Radically different.

Moore: Especially if you add that in Newspeak it's not only the number of words that is lost. The range of meaning for any specific word remaining in the eleventh edition will also be cut.

Locke: How could that be?

Moore: Take the word 'free'. Syme reckoned by 2050 – the date set for the final adoption of Newspeak – no individual would know that 'free' once excited ideas around being 'politically free' or 'intellectually free'.

Locke: But the word 'free' would still appear in the eleventh, final, edition of the Newspeak dictionary?

Moore: True. But only in the restricted sense of 'This dog is free from lice.' Or 'This field is free from weeds.' 'Free from' in Newspeak is 'without' – no 'Free to think for yourself.' That in Newspeak would be a 'thoughtcrime'.

Locke: An example of 'crimethink'?

Moore: You've got it. You're mastering Newspeak! Syme, if you remember, had two approaches to narrowing the range of thought. One, reduce the number of words: words such as 'honour', 'justice', 'morality', 'democracy', 'science', 'religion', simply ceased to exist. And two, reduce the range of meaning for any one word. We just saw what happened to 'free'.

Locke: No one would feel free to express regret at the loss of words because, as I understand Orwell, Newspeak is the tool of a

State that wants its citizens, for sinister undisclosed reasons, to have little or no capacity to think for themselves. The rulers' aim it seems to me is to try to control the public mind by regimenting their ideas. In pursuit of that aim they need the available language to be rigidly controlled.

Moore: As Syme put it: 'to narrow the range of possible thought.'

Locke: As Chomsky on the theme of thought control helped put it in *Manufacturing Consent*. Right. So I can best look at Newspeak as an experiment in implanting specific meanings in minds in an attempt to control public opinion.

Moore: Yes, but isn't it an attempt doomed to failure? On your view surely it can't be done.

Locke: Absolutely not. As I noted in Book III, 'the great Augustus himself, in Possession of that power which ruled the World, … could not arbitrarily appoint what *Idea* any Sound should be a sign of in the Mouths and common Language of his Subjects.'

Moore: What Augustus couldn't do, Orwell's Oceania couldn't do either.

Locke: No, but Newspeak's Syme absolutely presupposes he can. That's what makes it intriguing.

Moore: You mean because Newspeak is challenging your belief that ultimately each of us has no choice but to create our own meanings – that meanings for every single one of us are in the last resort private and subjective.

Locke: Exactly. Meanings are creatures of our own making. You remember I argued in Book III that 'Since one Man's Mind couldn't pass into another Man's Body' we could never have direct access to the private meanings another individual gives to the public words we share. Our meanings for words are bound to vary to some degree at least because our experience of life on which we base our meanings is varied.

Moore: And therefore the 'ideas' we bundle together to form our own meanings may be similar but are unlikely to be identical to the bundle others form.

Locke: Highly unlikely. But that's where Newspeak wants to differ. Syme and his cronies were attempting to manipulate the way we make meanings for ourselves, to try to make sure we all entertained the same meaning. That's specifically what intrigued me. They believed they could ensure the meanings we create are just the meanings Oceania's rulers wanted their subjects to have.

Moore: You make it sound like semantic fascism!

Locke: In a way it is. The opposite view – my view, a view the Newspeak advocates would fear most – is that we are free to make any meanings we wish.

Moore: One well-known individual held the extreme freedom view – Humpty Dumpty!

Locke: Humpty Dumpty? I don't recall a philosopher with that name.

Moore: Humpty Dumpty was a creation of that profound, riddling humourist Lewis Carroll. Carroll made Humpty a radical semanticist, who held the view that a word meant only what he decided it should mean. Carroll's heroine, a young girl called Alice, was dumbfounded by Humpty Dumpty's meaning for the word 'glory'.

Locke: And what did 'glory' mean for Mr Humpty Dumpty?

Moore: 'A nice knock-down argument.' That's what he said. Alice naturally was outraged. She objected: 'But "glory" doesn't mean 'a nice knock-down argument.' To which Humpty Dumpty classically retorted: 'When I use a word it means just what I choose it to mean – neither more nor less.'

Locke: Alice was right to be outraged.

Moore: Yes, well, he got his comeuppance. He fell off his wall. And, despite the King's promise, all the King's horses and all the King's men couldn't put Humpty together again!

Locke: No wonder. It's an untenable position if Mr Dumpty wants to live in a society, either Oceania or yours. Living in a society we have to create our meanings in the context of circumstances offered by that society. We experience not just its current circumstances, but also the circumstances inherited from its past. We're told stories about the heroic and tragic events of our society. So, inescapably, the public words we individually process are embedded in a context, a complex web of shared circumstances. That's why the individual meanings we create can be similar to other people's. Where I suppose the rulers of Oceania might hope to make an impact on our meanings for words is by directly affecting our beliefs about those circumstances.

Moore: That's exactly what they tried. Do you recall the obligatory attendance at the daily Hate Goldstein sessions on the telescreen.

Locke: I do. Particularly the effect they had on Winston. Orwell has him swinging from one mood to another. At one moment he writes, 'his heart went out to the lonely, derided heretic on the screen, sole guardian of truth and sanity in a world of lies.' And yet at the very next instant he continues, 'he was at one with the people about him and all that was said of Goldstein seemed to him to be true. And at that moment his secret loathing of Big Brother changed into adoration.'

Moore: Winston's mood swings are telling examples of the rulers influencing the way words embedded in a society are to be understood.

Locke: And Newspeak's task is to provide a language that expresses one truth: Goldstein is evil – to be passionately hated.

Moore: With Winston I suppose we do see the rulers succeeding up to a point. Yet regardless of how much they might affect the circumstances in which words were encountered, it would still remain true, wouldn't it, that arriving at meanings is still an individual act, the result of intricate processes at work in an individual's mind?

Locke: True enough, but it still remains the case that the experience being processed by each individual in their own minds is provided by society. Clearly the aim of the rulers of Oceania is to influence and, if possible, determine the nature of that experience and have it coded in the severely impoverished language they call Newspeak. If such an attempt were ever to succeed, human beings wouldn't any longer be human.

Moore: In what way?

Locke: To be human is to be capable of doubt, to experience uncertainty, to wish to question, to demand evidence.

Moore: In short, for Newspeak to work, Syme and his team need human beings to be dehumanised.

Locke: Doesn't that follow from the foundations of Newspeak? Its absolute presupposition is that having access to few words with fixed meanings will entail a narrowing of the range of thought. To this end Syme was trying to devise a language where the meanings of words were always certain. To achieve that certainty Syme was striving for the ultimate, simple linguistic equation: one word equals one and only one true meaning.

Moore: And that this one true meaning was to be specified by the rulers and somehow implanted in everyone's mind. So if we compare you and Syme: you presume we grow our own meanings for words depending on our own experience. It follows that our understanding of the meanings of the words others use is necessarily, not accidentally, uncertain. We can never really be totally sure. You accept inherent indeterminacy of word meaning and build from there.

Syme, by way of Newspeak, implicitly denies uncertainty is intrinsic to language in use and strives instead to implant certainty of meaning.

Locke: Absolutely. That's the fundamental difference as far as meaning goes. I live with uncertainty. Syme denies it.

Moore: It's worse than that though, isn't it? Newspeak isn't just about making determinate the meanings of the few words left in the dictionary in order to reduce uncertainty and improve control. Newspeak is the tool of a ruling party, out to destroy the capacity of its subjects to think and question for themselves, basically by controlling experience and confining language.

Locke: Yes, but it's a tool Orwell makes us see will not, cannot do the job. He shows us that more radical, non-linguistic measures are needed to break Winston's resistance to Newspeak. Syme's dream of one word equals one meaning will not of itself compel Winston to toe the party line.

Moore: You mean that even with a heavily reduced language what Syme called 'thoughtcrime' would still be possible?

Locke: Yes. Words are epiphenomenal. They trigger processes in the mind, but they don't entirely shape them. Having a reduced vocabulary isn't what narrows the range of thought. It's not having an independent mind – a mind that's critical, a mind with a relish for truth. Winston, Orwell shows us, had signs of such an independent mind, at least some of the time. That's the reason O'Brien, on behalf of the Party, had to have him mentally destroyed.

Moore: Orwell's bleak message to us is that in Oceania Winston's fate will be the fate of anyone who dares, despite the limited language, to think for themselves.

Locke: Even bleaker to me is Orwell's insight into the way people in general collude with the state and just accept their fate. They actively don't want to know the truth. They prefer the comfort of unknowing. Winston's neighbour, Parsons, is an example of someone perfectly happy not to think, question, criticise Newspeak. What makes Newspeak so sinister is what has happened to Parsons – the way he has become like your computationally controlled robots – responding to language in one way only, never misunderstanding, never confused, never uncertain of the meaning of a word. Give me a degree of misunderstanding any day!

Moore: At least it's human! Instead of responding to words like the monotone Daleks – 'exterminate, exterminate, exterminate'.

Locke: Daleks? Who are they?

Moore: I'll introduce you to them some day.

Locke: Right. But more pertinently Winston was not initially like Parsons, not totally adoring Big Brother. However, once his mind was destroyed, he finally adored like the best of them, adding a gin-soaked tear. The truth is the use of Newspeak demands what human nature, because of its innate variations, cannot normally give – totally uniformity of response. Through Newspeak the ruling Party was vainly hoping not only to outlaw any freedom of expression, but also any divergent interpretation of any statement they issued.

Moore: So if the Party claimed, as it did, that it had invented aeroplanes, it was true. Not historically true, or evidentially true, or provable, just true because the Party said so.

Locke: Winston feared the day the Party would declare 'two plus two equals five' and be believed!

Moore: Winston's tragedy was to be on the cusp. He could still recall an approach to the world expressed in a language diametrically opposed to Newspeak. An approach expressed in Thomas Jefferson's famous *Declaration of Independence* in Oldspeak, Standard English:

> We hold these truths to be self-evident, that all Men are created equal, that they are endowed by their Creator with certain inalienable Rights, that among these are Life, Liberty and the pursuit of Happiness. That to secure these Rights, Governments are instituted among Men, deriving their just powers from the consent of the governed.

Locke: You and I go along happily with the spirit of that declaration. Especially the bit about the government's powers being derived from the consent of the governed. I recall saying something like that myself in my *Two Treatises of Government*. But for the ruling Party of Oceania such language must be reduced to gibberish.

Moore: Because any such declaration is inimical to Oceania's world view. Suppose Winston were to try to translate the Jeffersonian declaration into Newspeak.

Locke: Again impossible. Anyone attempting a translation would be guilty, to use the language of Newspeak, of 'crimethought'. The penalty of which Winston knew only too well.

Moore: Do you think Orwell saw the implications of Newspeak for humanity if ever it were to become the standard language of Oceania?

Locke: Possibly, but I don't think that was his fundamental point. I suspect 'doublethink', 'thoughtcrime', 'duckspeak', were a verbal game for Orwell. The appendix to *1984* where he lists the Newspeak vocabulary seems to me a tongue-in-cheek *'jeu d'esprit.'* What I think Orwell was really exploring, judging by Winston's recurring anguish, was the way a debased language like Newspeak might make it impossible ever to know the truth about anything. That's an anguish I can resonate with.

Moore: I'm of course with you. Just imagine we could never prove anything, never examine any counter-evidence.

Locke: Which was exactly Winston's situation. He could never prove the Party had lied, falsified, misled its subjects because there were no records. The words of yesterday's alleged truth had always been erased.

Moore: Not so much erased as incinerated. Recall those flames burning in the enormous furnaces in the cellars of the Ministry of Truth.

Locke: There's a passage I thought was pivotal to Winston's anguish. Do you recall him realising that,

> when memory failed and written records were falsified – when that happened the claim of the Party to have improved the conditions of life had got to be accepted, because there didn't exist, and never again could exist, any standard against which it could be tested.

Moore: That indeed was his nightmare – not being able prove anything because there was never any hard evidence. It had all turned to ash.

Locke: What Winston lacked is something I believe is essential for establishing some idea of truth and that is discourse, conversation. We establish what we call truths by talking, comparing notes, comparing observations with each other, checking our evidence. That's the way we learn to adjust the meanings of our own words and our understanding of the words others use. Winston couldn't do that. In Oceania he was a kind of intellectual Robinson Crusoe, unable through talk with others to adjust his meanings.

Moore: You mean Winston had no opportunity to test his strands of meaning for public words against the strands others had in mind?

Locke: Ah! Your strand approach to meaning again.

Moore: As we discussed earlier I took it from your own knot-and-bundle image. The word, you wrote, was the knot tying together a loose bundle of ideas. I wrote some strands we gain, some we lose.

Locke: At least your strand approach allows for meanings to be perpetually changing. Individuals do add and subtract strands as their experience broadens. Change is the natural condition of meanings.

Moore: Constant change. 'Spam' and 'mouse' are just two examples of words that have taken on new strands of meaning for me over recent years.

Locke: Whereas Newspeak sought to stifle the intrinsic nature of semantic change. That's one of its basic flaws. I have a question for you. Is Oceania just a writer's fantasy? Does it bear any resemblance to your world today?

Moore: The resemblance was precisely Orwell's point. When *1984* was first published in 1949 readers were likely to believe Oceania was a lightly veiled portrait of totalitarian communism in the USSR. I certainly did. Re-reading it now, as you are reading it, reminds me that Oceania still has lessons for the West today.

Locke: Isn't that exactly the point Chomsky makes in his book *Necessary Illusions: Thought Control in Democratic Societies*? I see why you wanted me to read about his propaganda model.

Moore: I'm glad you read it. We pride ourselves in the West in believing ours is a free society. Making Chomsky's subtitle *Thought Control in Democratic Societies* all the more arresting.

Locke: But is there any real resemblance between your society and Oceania? You don't have thought police, you don't incinerate records, you don't vaporise dissidents.

Moore: No, we don't vaporise, nor tailor our instruments of torture the way Winston's rat cage was tailored. But our interrogators of alleged terrorists reportedly make use of pretty brutish tools of torture in pursuit of confessions. You do remember we discussed 'waterboarding'?

Locke: I remember. But you don't incinerate records, do you? Unlike Winston's frustration in seeking truth, you can always turn to evidence.

Moore: Which might have been redacted.

Locke: Redacted?

Moore: Made palatable for publication. No, our real frustration is over the often subtle way the Government and the media spin the evidence.

Locke: 'Spin'. That's new to me. Explain!

Moore: 'Spin' has become the common term for the practice of selecting the positive evidence supporting a case, a policy, a story, and largely ignoring the negative evidence. The users of 'spin' aim to persuade us to agree to whatever is being proposed. Engineering conformity has become a modern art! Its best practitioners are often in the public relations industry.

Locke: There's little new in that. I recall Blaise Pascal writing about the way certain biblical terms were construed to serve an interpretation.

Moore: Ours is not just a case of scholarly debate. 'Spin' has become so rife it's leading to a breakdown of trust in what the authorities and the media say, both written and spoken.

Locke: If it's true that 'spin' is undermining trust in what institutions or individuals say, you are heading for a very serious problem. Language is built on trust. It can only work as I once said as, 'the great Instrument and common Tye of Society' if people in general trust that the meanings of words other use are honestly meant. If 'spin' leads to distrust, we might as well become Trappists.

Moore: But how do we protect ourselves against 'spin'? How do we defeat the engineers of conformity?

Locke: There's only one way, and it's by going back to the fundamentals. Being aware of how manipulation is possible. Awareness is the only real shield against your engineers of spin. One of the fundamentals it's vital to keep in mind is the critical role 'Secret Reference' plays in all and every use of language.

Moore: Of course. We keep returning to 'Secret Reference' as your counter to our essential semantic individualism.

Locke: Which I trust you recall is not the same as your Humpty Dumpty's semantic solipsism. What I said in Book III was, 'Words in their primary or immediate Signification, stand for nothing, but the Ideas in the Mind of him that uses them'.

Moore: Which seems to make us primarily semantic individualists, underscoring your stress on the ultimately private and subjective nature of meanings.

Locke: Ultimately yes. But don't overlook the role of 'Secret Reference'. Universally we secretly refer – or as you would doubtless prefer to say, tacitly suppose – that the words we use excite the same meanings in the minds of others as they do in ours. That tacit belief – the first 'Secret Reference' – involves an act of implicit trust in the goodwill of others. Violating that trust may untune language as 'the great Instrument and common Tye of Society'.

Moore: Untune it because we may no longer be able to tacitly trust that each of us filters language in roughly the same way with roughly the same results.

Locke: Right. Too much 'spin' as you describe it can corrode that trust. Cause you to begin to seriously doubt what others say or write.

Moore: It's curious how different we are in some ways from Winston. His anguish was about never having any evidence for or against the state's statements.

Locke: Whereas your worry seems to be distrust of their statements because you fear their words are spun away from the truth.

Moore: Distrust debilitates. It breeds an insidious cynicism about the language of the state and of the media. In place of an impoverished language like Newspeak, we have a rich language, but we no longer instinctively trust its users.

Locke: Newspeak was an experiment that was bound to fail. Meanings grow in minds, they adapt, they change, they're not Newspeak's unchanging mono-meanings. But natural language can fail too unless it's backed by trust and a relish for truth as best we know it.

Moore: On that hope it's time for a break, I think.

Locke: I agree!

Conversation Eight

'The two Fountains of Knowledge from whence all the *Ideas* we have, or can naturally have, do spring.'
Book II
An Essay Concerning Human Understanding

Locke: An Empiricist?

Locke's double 'Secret Reference' depends very much on his view of the nature of mind, especially on the fundamental concept of 'Idea'. In this conversation we delve further into Locke's view of the mind and its workings. In particular I want to ask him what he makes of the widespread and inveterate canard about his epistemology.

It has become a commonplace to state that Locke is an empiricist, even the 'Father of Empiricism'. Yet Locke vigorously rebuts the charge by drawing a vital distinction between two different kinds of innateness. One kind of innateness he inveighs against, the other he welcomes with open arms.

His rebuttal focuses on the distinction he draws between innate principles and innate faculties. Locke does not, as is commonly alleged, view the mind as a *tabula rasa*. The rebuttal, however, turns out to be much more than an argument with those critics who appear not to recognise just how fundamental an innatist he is. For Locke the charge of empiricism amounts to an implicit attack on one of his most cherished convictions: that we should think for ourselves. His was the voice of the independent mind.

Moore: You're fuming, steaming. What's happened to that cool, disciplined reflection I so admire in you?

Locke: I've just been reading books about me in your library. I never would have believed I could be so misunderstood! By philosophers, by historians of philosophy, by encyclopaedists. They've all got it completely wrong.

Moore: No wonder you're fuming. What exactly have they misunderstood?

Locke: Where I stand on the mind. They all charge me with being an out-and-out empiricist. Or worse, in the encyclopaedia, the 'Father of British Empiricism'. Simply because I attack one very particular kind of innatism they seem to assume I'm against any idea of a mind endowed with innate faculties. Over and over again they claim one of my central arguments in the *Essay* is that the human mind is a blank slate. You even own a book whose title is *The Blank Slate*. 'Tabula rasa' is another phrase they attribute to me more times than I've had hot luncheons. Isn't that the modern expression?

Moore: Not quite, but I get your drift.

Locke: I do know someone who referred to the mind as a 'tabula rasa', but it wasn't me. Can you manage another bit of Latin?

Moore: As I said earlier, in my day you had to pass a Latin exam to be allowed into Cambridge.

Locke: Then you'll understand Thomas Aquinas. In his *Summa Theologica,* Thomas wrote, 'Intellectus autem humanus … est sicut tabula rasa in qua nihil est scriptum.'

Moore: The human mind is a blank slate on which nothing is written.

Locke: Good enough. But here's a challenge: find me describing the mind as a 'tabula rasa' anywhere in the *Essay*.

Moore: I'm not picking up that gauntlet. A toothcomb search I tried some time ago failed utterly to produce either a 'tabula rasa' or a 'blank slate' anywhere in *An Essay Concerning Human Understanding*.

Locke: Exactly!

Moore: However, I did spot something that might begin to explain how the popular misconception might have arisen.

Locke: Ah?

Moore: It was something you wrote at the beginning of Book II about the mind and white paper. But first I want to try and dispel your gloom about how history has treated you. The fact is that not everyone has misunderstood you.

Locke: You mean there are some enlightened ones?

Moore: One of them is Thomas Ebenezer Webb.

Locke: Thomas who? Never heard of him.

Moore: I admit he's not all that well known as a philosopher. But in the mid-nineteenth century he wrote an essay entitled *The Intellectualism of Locke*. I suspect you'd appreciate his opening sentence. How good is your French?

Locke: I can manage, thank you!

Moore: He begins, 'What if the Empiricism of Locke be one of the 'fables convenues' of Philosophy?' And then goes on to add, 'This is the fact which it is the object of this essay to establish, and it is on the establishment of this fact that I rest Locke's claim to be regarded as a great thinker.' That's Webb's opening salvo!

Locke: Obviously a great philosopher – clearly a man who thought his own thoughts. He at least must have recognised how significant for my view of how the mind works were its innate operations – operations springing, I wrote, from the fountain of reflection. I must read this essay.

Moore: I'll see if I can get you a copy. But he wasn't the only one. I realise you're not a fan of Leibniz, but I don't believe he would ever have labelled you as an empiricist.

Locke: Because?

Moore: The reason's in a letter he wrote – I forget to whom – in which there's a succinct one-sentence summary of your view of the mind.

Locke: I'd like to hear that sentence.

Moore: It's in Latin!

Locke: I think I can manage!

Moore: It runs, 'Nihil est in intellectu quod non fuerit prius in sensu, nisi ipse intellectus.'

Locke: Nothing is in the mind that was not first in the senses, except the mind itself. Nisi ipse intellectus. Leibniz, like the inestimable Webb, seems to recognise I saw the mind as innately endowed to reflect on its own processes. I still can't understand why everyone else could get it so wrong. Don't you think my second fountain, the fountain of reflection, spelled it out clearly enough?

Moore: I do now. But I didn't always grasp the subtlety of your ideas. It was only after a close reading of the *Essay* that I began to see how your enquiry into the original, certainty and extent of human knowledge depended upon your two fountains, the fountain of sensation and the fountain of reflection, continuously interacting. From the start you had them working in tandem.

Locke: In tandem. I like that. You're right of course. The two fountains are interacting all the time, feeding off each other. The mind's innate operations are needed to work with the experiences the senses provide. For instance, ideas we come to name 'heat', 'cold', 'soft', 'hard', 'bitter', 'sweet' are a consequence of the workings of the mind.

Moore: You saw the role of the sensation as initiating, triggering innate processes in the mind.

Locke: Triggering, yes. But I never claimed the triggering in any way determined the directions the mind's operations took. More importantly the interaction between the two fountains is an ongoing process. If you must have a label, call me an interactionist!

Moore: I will, but I suspect the empiricist label has stuck because of something you wrote. You did say, did you not, that all knowledge comes from experience?

Locke: I did. It was my one-word answer to my own rhetorical question: where does all our knowledge come from?

Moore: We're now talking about how your answer was understood. You, above all, know we're on a risk gradient trying to understand the language of another – sometimes we get it right, sometimes disastrously wrong. You knew what you had in mind by 'experience'. Your idea embraced both what comes to us via the senses and from innate operations of the mind. But if you were understood to mean simply responses to the world from the senses, then crudely you're going to be labelled an empiricist, deriving all knowledge from one fountain, the fountain of sensation. You did after all lay a lot of stress on 'experience' in places.

Locke: Where exactly?

Moore: Let me read you a passage from Book II: 'All those sublime Thoughts, which tower above the Clouds, and reach as high as Heaven itself, take their Rise and Footing here (in Experience)'.

Locke: Be fair. Don't stop. 'In those remote Speculations, … it stirs not one jot beyond those Ideas, which Sense or Reflection, have offered for its Contemplation.' Sense and Reflection. Not just one but both.

Moore: I realise that now. For you the combination of sensory and reflective experience is essential if any knowledge is ever to be gained. Perhaps you didn't lay enough stress on the role of the fountain of reflection.

Locke: Perhaps.

Moore: I said a bit earlier I'd spotted something you wrote that may be responsible for the enduring label 'empiricist'. You do recall the statement about the mind and white paper.

Locke: It wasn't a statement, it was a supposition. I never claimed the mind was like white paper. What I did in Book I was challenge what was at the time a received doctrine: that men have innate principles and innate ideas, not based on prior experience, stamped on their minds.

Moore: I shouldn't have said 'statement'. I should have said 'conjecture'.

Locke: Right. An Aunt Sally of a conjecture, you might say. Is that right?

Moore: Something put up to knock down. Yes.

Locke: Good. What I wrote was *if* – *if* we were to suppose the mind were like white paper, then I argued we would have a serious problem. It would be impossible to explain how all the ideas, fanciful as well as reasonable, we come to have ever arose. Ergo the conjecture is false. The mind is not like white paper; it must be endowed with its own innate operations.

Moore: Perhaps here we're getting close to the source of the popular misconception of you as a champion empiricist. Book I of the *Essay* is commonly read as a sustained diatribe against innateness. But actually you are supporting it up to the hilt.

Locke: Book I is a bit of a tirade I admit against one kind of innateness. But one kind only. Distinctions, distinctions. You must distinguish between two kinds of innateness. One I will attack with the last breath of my body, the other I will defend to the death.

Moore: I sometimes think the imperative 'Distinguish' should be carved on your headstone. Teach me to distinguish between the useful and the useless kinds of innateness.

Locke: Basically for me the crucial distinction lies between those whose camp is erected on the belief that principles and notions are innate, and those like myself who believe the mind has no innate principles or notions but is innately endowed with operations, processes. Lord Herbert is a good example of the first camp.

Moore: Lord Herbert of Cherbury believed we're hardwired with innate principles and ideas.

Locke: 'Hardwired'! That's new to me. I like it. Yes. His *De Veritate* is a clear example of those who claim principles are hardwired, imprinted on the mind. In Book I, the innateness I worked hard to subvert was the established opinion among some thinkers that human beings are born knowing things about the world.

Moore: Whereas your view of innateness was ...?

Locke: I believed what was hardwired were faculties, the capacity to abstract from the particular, for example, and dispositions, to be curious, to be empathetic – that's a word I've learnt recently – they too were hardwired. Didn't your Chomsky propose that we are born with a universal grammar, making the brain in part a language acquisition device?

Moore: You're right, he did claim we were born with a LAD, that is with the necessary structures and neural pathways to develop a language. I have a cautionary note about how that claim has been misunderstood too, but maybe it's best for another time. Back to Lord Herbert. What specifically did Herbert believe was innate?

Locke: One of his principles was: 'Impossible est idem, et non esse'.

Moore: Roughly construed: it is impossible for the same thing to be, and not to be.

Locke: Not too rough. Another proposition often cited as an innate principle was: 'Whatever is, is.'

Moore: True enough.

Locke: Truth alone is not sufficient to establish innateness. The confusion I argued lay in treating what is universally accepted as equivalent to innately given. Universal consent can be arrived at by other ways.

Moore: By the use of reason for instance?

Locke: Exactly. Granted the principle 'What is, is' is self-evident, but that's not necessarily because it is inscribed, hardwired, on our brains. Rather it's because any consideration of the nature of things excited by those words would not permit a reader to think otherwise, how or whensoever he is brought to reflect on them. I believe it's moral rules that most readily undermine the idea of innate principles inscribed on our minds. Take as one example: parents preserve and cherish their children. Is this supposed to be an innate rule that directs the actions of us all? Or else a truth all of us have imprinted upon our minds?

Moore: Do we have to re-visit those grisly tales you told of the inhabitants of Mingrelia and Peru in ancient times?

Locke: Well, the ancient Mingrelians are reported to have buried their children alive, and the Peruvians, so Garcilaso de la Vega claims, fattened and ate the children they had with their female captives and …

Moore: Right, right, your point is made. Moral principles are matters for cultures. Not all parents live in cultures where the morality demands they universally preserve and cherish their children. It's said the Spartans placed their babes on the roof at night to see if they were robust enough to survive.

Locke: I never imagined that was a Greek practice.

Moore: I sense for you, however, there's something deeper, more fundamental involved in the issue of what is and what is not to count as innate. Isn't it much more than an intellectual disagreement about what exactly we should believe is innately imprinted?

Locke: You're right of course. It's not so much these claims themselves that disturb me as the consequences for our conduct that may follow. Professing innate principles lends considerable powers to the professors.

Moore: In what way?

Locke: Consider the role of a teacher. Consider what power he gains once he firmly believes there are principles innately inscribed on our minds and he knows what they are.

Moore: I recall now. You bring Book I to a close with a moving and cogent philippic against authoritarian teaching.

Locke: I don't remember exactly. I believe I did.

Moore: Let me quote you:

> It was of no small advantage to those who affected to be Masters and Teachers, to make this the Principle of Principles, That Principles must not

> be questioned: For having once established this Tenet, that there are innate Principles, it put their Followers upon a necessity of receiving some Doctrines as such; which was to take them off from the use of their own Reason and Judgement, and put them upon believing and taking them upon trust, without farther examination ...

Locke: I recall the passage now. It runs on: 'In which posture of blind credulity, they might be more easily governed by, and made useful to some sort of Men, who had the skill and office to principle and guide them'.

Moore: 'A posture of blind credulity', I've long cherished that phrase. But you haven't finished your appeal to the independent mind. It's not only teachers, but those in authority who benefit. 'Nor is it', you write:

> ... a small power it gives one Man over another, to have the Authority to be the Dictator of Principles, and Teacher of unquestionable Truths; and to make a Man swallow that for an innate Principle, which may serve to his purpose, who teacheth them.

Magnificent!

Locke: It's what I believe. We should strive to think for ourselves.

Moore: After reading it, I composed a maxim for myself and for my students: 'Suspend judgement, examine the evidence.'

Locke: I never said that. I wish I had. I could have made it an epigraph for my book *Some Thoughts on Education.*

Moore: So to return to innatism. The innatism Book I derides is the innatism that assumes we are innately endowed with principles and notions. The innatism you favour assumes the mind is innately endowed not with principles and notions but with certain operations.

Locke: Specifically the ones I discuss under the fountain of reflection. One of the most important of those operations is, as I said, our ability to abstract, to quit particulars. Your Chomsky, again I think, if I read *Cartesian Linguistics* right, would agree when he writes about our freedom from stimuli.

Moore: He certainly makes the point very strongly that our use of language shows us to be stimulus free, not stimulus-bound, beings. So we can conclude you're not an empiricist, certainly not the 'Father of Empiricism'. By what title should I call you?

Locke: Since I hold the way to understanding lies through the powers of our minds working in tandem with the organs of our bodies, how about in your language calling me an interactionist, or, if you prefer, on some days an empirical rationalist, on others, a rational empiricist?

Moore: An oxymoron will do fine to end on. Till next time.

Conversation Nine

John Locke and Damaris Masham, née Cudworth: Questions of Influence

This conversation delves into Locke's personal life, and in particular, his relationship with the woman who may have been the love of his life. That woman was Damaris Masham who has been described as 'the woman philosopher of her age'. Her best known works, published anonymously, were *A Discourse Concerning the Love of God*, 1696, and *Occasional Thoughts in Reference to a Vertuous or Christian Life*, 1705. To some scholars her ideas, radical for her time, are the ideas of an early feminist. Her correspondents besides Locke included Leibniz. Damaris was 23 years old and Locke 49 when they first met in 1681. Before she married Sir Francis Masham, a widower with eight children, Damaris was a Cudworth, a daughter of Ralph Cudworth, the eminent Cambridge Platonist.

In this conversation John Locke and Terence Moore discuss questions of influence. Initially, as one might expect, the focus is on Locke's influence on the language of Damaris' work. But more surprisingly, Locke turns the tables and reflects on Damaris' influence on his own ideas. It helps to know that the last decade of his life was spent in her company in her family home at Oates in Essex, and that this last decade was for him immensely productive. He remained at Oates until his death on 28th October 1704. Locke's French translator, Pierre Coste, a contemporary of theirs, reports that Damaris was by his side, reading to him from the Psalms when he died.

As well as exploring their influence on each other's work, the conversation attempts, tentatively, to probe the nature of their relationship. In the early days, before Damaris Cudworth married

Sir Francis Masham, the links seem clearly romantic. Pastoral poems and discreet love letters have come down to us in the eight volumes of E.S.de Beer's monumental work, *The Correspondence of John Locke*. Later, with Locke lodging at the Masham's home, their attachment to each other appears to have grown and deepened.

Moore: I want to talk to you this evening about influence, specifically yours on Damaris Masham.

Locke: (**Sighs.**) Damaris! The light and love of my life!

Moore: (**Smiles.**) I've always imagined that might be the case. But let's start with how much you influenced her work. She was after all, some say, among the best women philosophers of her time.

Locke: And a brilliant thinker. To be honest I'm not at all sure how much influence I actually had. I certainly encouraged her to publish her writings, but remember she was the daughter of Ralph Cudworth, author of *The True Intellectual System of the Universe*. It was really from her I learnt to appreciate some aspects of his work. I suspect she may have remained under her father's influence more than mine.

Moore: Interesting you should have mentioned Cudworth. I have a link, admittedly tenuous, with him.

Locke: How's that?

Moore: He was Master of my College at one point.

Locke: Clare! I recall him as Master at Christ's College.

Moore: That is true. But he was at Clare, Clare Hall, as it was known then, from 1645 to 1654. In the end he left us for Christ's. But let's return to the question of your influence on Damaris.

Locke: What makes you think I might have had some influence on her?

Moore: A number of reasons. For a start, living in the Mashams' house, Oates, you were free to discuss her ideas with her whenever you both wished. This at the very time she was writing *A Discourse Concerning the Love of God.* and her *Occasional Thoughts in Reference to a Vertuous or Christian Life*. Both incidentally published anonymously. Surely Oates was a breeding ground for influence!

Locke: True enough. I did reside at Oates for at least a decade, but only after we'd agreed terms – one pound a week for me and my servant's upkeep and a shilling a week for stabling my horse, Sorrell.

Moore: So, as I said, you and she were in a position to talk over ideas on a daily basis.

Locke: Except when her children and her household duties, which she didn't relish, called her away.

Moore: Furthermore Damaris cites you in both her works. And not only that, more significant than her citations was the reaction to her work. When *Occasional Thoughts* was published it was widely believed to have been written by you. Doesn't that suggest influence?

Locke: Possibly, but have you any real evidence?

Moore: Shreds of evidence, yes. For example, a letter has come down to us from a Richard Gwinnett to the poet Elizabeth Thomas. He writes praising, I quote, 'a little Posthumous Treatise of Mr Locke.' He goes on to note that the work is 'nothing inferior to the more elaborate Works of that Ingenious author.'

Locke: Thank him for 'Ingenious', but just because Gwinnett mistakenly attributed her work to me doesn't prove I influenced her.

Moore: It's suggestive though, isn't it? And it wasn't only *Occasional Thoughts*, it was also her *Discourse* that was attributed to you.

Locke: Who by this time?

Moore: Well, John Norris for one, Mary Astell for another.

Locke: Those two should have known better. Damaris never liked John very much. Not sure why. He always pretended to respect my ideas but was always critical of them, especially of *An Essay Concerning Human Understanding*.

Moore: He did dedicate two of his works to Lady Masham.

Locke: In that case he should have recognised the *Discourse* as her work not mine.

Moore: The evidence for your influence on her is not only misattribution, it's also, and I believe more importantly, her terminology. In *Occasional Thoughts* Damaris raises your epistemological question about the grounds of knowledge. Without quoting you she refers to 'Knowledge immediately received from Sense or Reflection.' She uses your exact terms. The very words you use in *An Essay Concerning Human Understanding* for your two fountains of knowledge.

Locke: Her father certainly wouldn't have approved of that! For Ralph Cudworth, God was firmly at the centre of 'The True Intellectual System'. Since he believed the human mind contains an imprint of the divine, our ideas had to be innate.

Moore: So would it be true to say that at the basis of Cudworth's epistemology was the idea that the human mind, however impaired, mirrors the mind of God?

Locke: You could say that. What I'd say is that Cudworth assumed the mind came furnished with ideas and knowledge. The mind certainly was not – what did they say I called it? – a *tabula rasa*. I, on the contrary, assumed all the ideas the mind came to have were the outcome of the workings of the fountains of sensation and reflection. Naturally a consequence of my view was that different minds could develop ideas differently depending upon their experience of the world.

Moore: And Damaris in *Occasional Thoughts* followed your account, not her father's.

Locke: True. I suppose you could call that influence.

Moore: *Occasional Thoughts* has other phrases expressing ideas her father would not have shared. Damaris describes the idea of God as 'a Proposition containing many complex ideas in it; and which we are not capable of framing till we have been long acquainted with pleasing Sensations.' Surely that could easily be a sentence from your *Essay*. You must be able to understand why you were believed to be the author. You are, after all, the man whose explanations invariably invoke ideas! Sometimes, simple, more often complex.

Locke: I can see what you are driving at! I have to admit you're building a case for some influence. But it's in both directions, mine on her, hers on me. It will only strengthen your case if I tell you she also made some helpful comments on the abridged version of the *Essay* I was writing while in Holland.

Moore: I recall a letter she wrote you in which she reports you asked her to point out any mistakes in the abridged version. No one does that unless they respect the person's judgement. I quote her, 'It will become me to show you your mistakes.' Signed, Philoclea.

Locke: Ah, Philoclea! That was the name she used in those early days before I had to flee to Holland – I didn't want to go but I had no choice. A warrant had been issued for my arrest. In those halcyon days Damaris and I would write poems to each other.

Moore: And wasn't your nom-de-plume Philander?

Locke: Indeed it was. But aren't you now really asking about her influence on me? After all, as you pointed out, I lived in her house for more than ten years, free to discuss ideas on a daily basis.

Moore: Of course I'm interested in her influence on you. But I also want you to agree that you did exert some influence on her writings.

Locke: Alright, I agree. Providing you agree that questions of the influence of philosopher X over philosopher Y are generally complex and fraught with difficulties, whoever they are.

Moore: I agree, agree wholeheartedly. However that decade at Oates was certainly a highly productive time for you.

Locke: Oates, tucked away in the Essex countryside, was a perfect refuge. During those years I revised the *Essay*, wrote a new chapter, 'Of Identity and Diversity' for Book II, made significant changes to the chapter 'Of Power', wrote three editions of *Some Thoughts Concerning Education*, wrote *The Reasonableness of Christianity* and more besides.

Moore: I was right then, that decade was productive! And Damaris was an influential part of that creativity. Your creativity.

Locke: You're right of course. But what makes you so sure?

Moore: Because you tell us. In the Preface to the Reader for *The Reasonableness of Christianity* you wrote – let me read it to you – 'The Wonderful Harmony … in all parts of the sacred History of the Gospel, was of no small Weight with me and another Person, who … every Day, asked me what more the Scripture had taught me.' That other Person, if we're frank, was Damaris, wasn't it?

Locke: Well, Damaris and I, as you know from her work, did share an abiding interest in both religious and philosophical questions.

Moore: We know too from a letter you sent to your great friend Philipp van Limborch about your respect for her judgement. You wrote that Damaris was, 'so much occupied with study and reflection on theological and philosophical matters that you could find few men with whom you might associate with greater profit and pleasure.' You added to crown it that 'her judgement is singularly keen', and you knew 'few men capable of discussing with such insight the most abstruse subjects, such as are beyond the grasp, I do not say of women, but even of the most educated men.'

Locke: Damaris was – how shall I put it – my closest companion during those years at Oates.

Moore: Closest companion! She puts it differently.

Locke: What do you mean?

Moore: In a letter to Leibniz she says of you that you have 'supplied to me the Place of a Father and Brother.' You are on record as writing to Damaris saying you regard her as 'a sister or a daughter, or something nearer than those relations.'

Locke: When did I write that?

Moore: Autumn, 1690, shortly before you moved into Oates permanently. And then, alas, of course the letters stopped. But tell me more about those early years, about Damaris as Philoclea. And what you had in mind by something nearer than the relation of a sister or a daughter.

Locke: I'll try to explain. But first I want you to understand how original, how independent Damaris' thinking was. Yes, of course there was influence, some influence at least, but Damaris had a mind of her own. It probably shone out best in her last work.

Moore: *Occasional Thoughts in Reference to a Vertuous or Christian Life*?

Locke: Yes. 'Vertuous' is the key. Why, Damaris pondered, should we try to lead a virtuous life?

Moore: The word 'vertuous' seems to have slipped out of common use these days. Certainly changed its spelling!

Locke: Interesting. Shall I rather say, lead a morally good life?

Moore: I guess we'd all be with you then.

Locke: Her favourite example involved a cat. She'd say when you see a cat tormenting a mouse it has caught, it doesn't make sense to say it's a bad cat, an immoral cat. But if a man was tormenting a cat you'd certainly condemn him. 'Why is that?' she'd ask rhetorically.

Moore: And answered?

Locke: Because human beings are free agents responsible for their actions. The cat is not.

Moore: So we are morally accountable because Damaris sees us as possessing free will, so able to choose for ourselves a virtuous course of action.

Locke: Free will is necessary but not of itself sufficient. Coupled with free will must be the power of reasoning. Damaris believed, as I do, that we are fundamentally free and reasoning agents. You may have noticed I changed my account of 'will' in the second edition of the *Essay*.

Moore: Written at Oates. Yes, I did notice. Before moving into Oates you construed the will as 'preferring any Action to its forbearance'. However in the second edition, written in Oates, your revised definition of will reads 'the Power of the Mind to determine its thought, to the producing, continuing, or stopping of any Action, as far as it depends on us'. This looks much more like self-conscious self-determination. Was that Damaris talking?

Locke: I can't claim Damaris didn't have some influence. Our talk often turned to the importance of the role of the will.

Moore: So it would be fair to say that as a result of your conversations you made changes to the *Essay*.

Locke: Damaris could put things more tellingly. We must, she wrote, be 'Masters of our own Actions' if we are to be accountable for them. Freedom to act is one essential condition for moral accountability. I agreed with her on that.

Moore: That we are free agents was easier to believe in your age than in mine.

Locke: Oh? Why?

Moore: Let's say for now that since the seventeenth century our intellectual climate has been changed considerably by some remarkable thinkers. But the fact that you and Damaris happened to agree on the grounds of moral accountability is not giving me clear evidence of her thinking independently. It sounds more like mutual influence.

Locke: True. As I said questions of influence are rarely straightforward. But whenever she was thinking as a practical moralist, she thought independently. She pushed the consequences of human beings possessing free will and reason much further than I ever did. Damaris wanted to edify.

Moore: But so did you. Three editions of *Some Thoughts Concerning Education*. Written at Oates.

Locke: Perhaps. But the level for me was personal. Damaris was much more radical, more general.

Moore: Explain.

Locke: In *Some Thoughts* I was simply trying to ensure that my close friends, the Clarkes, in bringing up their son Edward, achieved the right balance, the balance between knowing things and wanting to know things.

Moore: You put it somewhat more elegantly at the end of *Some Thoughts*. You wrote, 'The Tutor should remember that his Business is not so much to teach him all that is knowable, as to raise in him a love and esteem of Knowledge and to put him in the right way of knowing and improving himself when he has a Mind to do it.' By improving himself you meant gaining 'a Mastery over his Inclinations and submitting his Appetites to Reason.'

Locke: That's what I believe. Damaris though attacked a much more fundamental and widespread issue. She recognised that the capacity to choose, to act according to Reason, was in all of us frequently abused. Our appetites led us not to be 'Vertuous'. The remedy of the abuse she saw lay in early education. Who was best placed to ensure that her child grew up virtuous? Why, the mother, of course.

Moore: I have her words here. She wrote, 'Before we come to a Ripeness of Understanding … the assistance of Mothers is necessary to the making of men Vertuous.' It's an early call for the education of women.

Locke: I would never have written those words. It's more than a call. It's recognising that if women are to 'make men Vertuous' it is essential they themselves should have a solid education in the reasoning underpinning virtuous conduct. Damaris passionately believed that a harmonious society needed women just as much as men to have the opportunity to learn that the principles of virtue consist in being able, she would say, 'to govern our Passions and subject our Appetites to the directions of our Reason.'

Moore: Another phrase like yours in *Some Thoughts*!

Locke: Damaris, I insist, in pursuing the idea of education for women, was thinking her own thoughts, independent of me.

Moore: It seems she was what we would call an early feminist. She wasn't to know it would be several centuries before women were ever admitted to full status as students at Cambridge.

Locke: Shame on you! But what did you have in mind when you said earlier that it was easier in our time to believe that human beings are free agents? This was a notion central to both Damaris and me.

Moore: Well, the intellectual climate in which we currently live has in part been created by a number of radical thinkers, among them Darwin, Marx and Freud. The one that runs directly counter to your belief in us as free agents is Freud.

Locke: Freud? What did he have to say?

Moore: Freud's ideas have revolutionised the way we think about ourselves. Ways that profoundly affect your and Damaris' belief that we are morally accountable because we are 'Masters of our own Actions'.

Locke: A revolution! That sounds serious. What's the core of this revolution?

Moore: Difficult to summarise fairly, and doubtless I'll oversimplify, but I would say for me Freud's radical contribution is the idea that mental life is ultimately rooted in the Id and becomes conscious in the course of adapting, with the help of the Ego, to the world it finds itself in.

Locke: Id! Ego!

Moore: Sorry. I slipped into Freudese. They are terms of his art. Essentially construe Id as the most primitive and instinctive part of the unconscious. Freud, a thinker who tried to be systematic, believes our conscious choices, our Ego's decisions, judgements are influenced by events, experiences, often early in life, sometimes sexual – experiences we are not ordinarily conscious of. So any idea that we are 'Masters of our own Actions' seems, to put it mildly, far too confident of the independence of our conscious powers.

Locke: Intriguing. Let me see if I've got this right. This Freud is claiming that human behaviour is explicable only if processes going on within us, unconscious processes we are ordinarily unaware of, are taken into account.

Moore: That's a way of putting it.

Locke: I'm going to have to read some of your Freud.

Moore: I think you'll find his *Interpretation of Dreams* somewhere on my shelves.

Locke: But if we're not 'Masters of our own Actions' where's the foundation for our moral accountability? Damaris and I rested our case on our being 'free Agents'. But we are not free if Freud's unconscious is determining our actions.

Moore: Steady on. Let's get our words right. 'Influencing' you, a master of drawing distinctions, will recognise is not the same as 'determining'.

Locke: So what do you think?

Moore: Well, I'm a child of the climate Freud, Darwin and Marx helped to create, but I do believe we are, to an extent, free agents. But only free to a degree, and that degree may be a lot smaller than I recognise.

Locke: So what do you think determines the degree of freedom?

Moore: Self-awareness. For me self-awareness is all. And to gain self-awareness, one of the things we have to be prepared to do is look into our past experiences to try to glean some idea of what may be influencing, not determining, our present decisions and judgements.

Locke: I can see now why you balked at our notion of 'free Agents' as the foundation of moral judgements. For you then it must seem far too cavalier. I need to read some Freud.

Moore: Some you may resonate to, some not. I'm warning you. Some of his writings actually may bear on your view of Damaris as, I quote, 'a sister, or a daughter, or something nearer than those relations.' What did you have in mind by nearer than those relations? You were going to explain.

Locke: (**Hacking cough**.) Another time perhaps.

Moore: Take care of that cough of yours!

Conversation Ten

Exploring with Locke the Origins of Language

Down the centuries a Holy Grail for some linguists has been to discover the origins of language. The ancient Greek historian, Herodotus, fifth century BC, tells the story of a pharaoh's attempt to discover the first, original language. Psammetichus, a Phrygian, devised an experiment that required taking two new-born children and isolating them in an uninhabited region in the care of a shepherd. The shepherd was instructed not to speak a word in their hearing. Psammetichus hoped that the words the children first spoke, once past the age of babbling, would count as the world's original language. His hope was fulfilled when the shepherd reported both children had run towards him, stretching out their hands and calling 'bekos'. 'Bekos' was the Phrygian word for 'bread'. For Psammetichus it was Q.E.D.

In the seventeenth century a different view of the origins of language prevailed. Most of Locke's contemporaries believed the Grail was to be found in the first Book of Moses, entitled Genesis, Chapter 2, v. 19–20. There a prelapsarian Adam was pronounced the originator of language:

> And out of the ground the Lord God formed every beast of the field, and every fowl of the air; and brought them unto Adam to see what he would call them: and whatsoever Adam called every living creature, that was the name thereof. And Adam gave names to all cattle, and to the fowl of the air, and to every beast of the field.

Locke naturally knew the verses but did not agree with the views they expressed. To know is not to believe. Locke believed the links between words and meanings were not divinely inspired but necessarily arbitrary. This belief Locke was to discover from Moore was re-stated by the nineteenth-century Swiss linguist, popularly known as the 'Father of Modern Linguistics', Ferdinand de Saussure. The first of his two basic principles was: 'Principle 1: The Arbitrary Nature of the Sign.'

In this conversation Locke and Moore first discuss the shortcomings of the Adamic view, focusing on the inherently arbitrary nature of the links between words and the world. Subsequently Locke, finding Saussure's famous work, *Cours de Linguistique Générale* in Moore's library, takes the opportunity to express his disagreement with certain of Saussure's key ideas.

A man of fundamentals, Locke in his account of arbitrariness broadens and deepens its significance for our understanding of our actual use of language. Locke's work also foreshadows Saussure's second basic principle: 'Principle II: The Linear Nature of the Signifier'. Unlike Saussure, Locke goes on to explore the implications of linearity for the crucial distinction between the way we perceive and the way we must talk about what we perceive. For Locke the fact that perception is holistic and speech linear has far-reaching consequences both for the use and the understanding of each other's language.

Locke: If our topic for this evening is 'A Grail Abandoned', I first need to know precisely what this abandoned Grail is.

Moore: Of course. The Grail, as I understand it, is the quest for the origins of language.

Locke: And why do you say the Grail has been abandoned?

Moore: It was the Linguistic Society of Paris that did it. At their meeting in 1866 they expressly prohibited any discussion of the origins of language. Speculation was too wild, they said, too short of evidence, too unscientific. Gestures, natural cries, animal calls were all unproven contenders. Naturally the prohibition didn't have an immediate effect. But over time and with the ideas of Saussure a new issue, the systemic or structural nature of language became the focus of attention, leaving speculations on the origins of language to wither on the vine.

Locke: But if it's withered on the vine why do you want us to pursue it?

Moore: Because there was a particular view of the origins that was widespread in the seventeenth century and you didn't agree with it. The reasons you didn't agree tell me a great deal about your thoughts on the nature, use and signification of language. The widespread view in your century – a view as I say you didn't share – held that prelapsarian Adam was the original creator of language. We might call it the Adamic view. Human beings, many of your contemporaries believed, owed the origins of language to Adam, the first great name-giver!

Locke: You're thinking of the way the first book of Moses was interpreted. Genesis, Chapter II, verses 19–20. It runs, if my memory serves me well:

> Out of the ground the Lord God formed every beast of the field, and every fowl of the air; and brought them unto Adam to see what he would call them: and whatsoever Adam called every living creature, that was the name thereof.

Moore: I'm impressed. Your memory is certainly serving you well. Although few nowadays would subscribe to the Genesis account of the origins of language, many would, perhaps unwittingly, accept its tacit underlying assumption.

Locke: Its tacit underlying assumption being …?

Moore: That language is essentially a naming process.

Locke: They'd be wrong, of course. Whatever our definition of language is, it is, as we have discussed, not a simple naming process.

Moore: Yet I suspect that widespread view in your time did firmly believe it was. What's also interesting is that it reminds me that in the seventeenth-century literate individuals had two significant books to read: one was the Holy Bible and the other what we might call the Book of Nature, the Book Boyle, Newton, you and the other Fellows of the recently founded Royal Society for the Improving of Natural Knowledge were busily writing. Yet you clearly knew the first Book well too.

Locke: To know is not necessarily to believe.

Moore: But many surely did. Take your friend from school days Robert South. He was enthusiastic about Adam's linguistically creative act. At the very least it resolved for him as it did for others the question of the origins of language.

Locke: It's true. Robert and I were both at Westminster. But he was a couple of years younger than me. Yes, Robert was a man of the Church who believed the Genesis account of the origins of language and praised Adam to the skies.

Moore: I have here a passage of a sermon South once preached at St. Paul's that supports your view of him. Let me read it to you.

> Adam came into the world a philosopher, which sufficiently appeared by his writing the nature of things upon their names; he could view essences in themselves, … An Aristotle was but a rubbish of an Adam, and Athens but the rudiments of Paradise.

Locke: I never thought of Robert as a philosopher of language. My concern with the views he expressed was that he was always inclined to take words literally. What mattered for Robert and for those who shared his views was that the relation between word and object was divine, God-given.

Moore: You of course didn't agree.

Locke: No I didn't. The trouble with Robert's lot was that they acted as if the Bible authorised for all time the view that Adam's words for the names of the beasts of the field and the fowl of the air also carried with them the knowledge of each species and its essence.

Moore: Can I put that another way? According to Robert, Adam, in giving names to the beasts of the field and the fowl of the air, was doing a lot more than just naming them. Words were not just vocal labels. Adam, Robert claimed, was also 'writing the nature of things upon their names' and was able to 'view their essences in themselves'. On this view Adam's language, believed to be Hebrew, was an essential source of knowledge of the nature of things.

Locke: So they believed. What they didn't take into account were two fundamental shortcomings in their approach. First, as you said, they treated language as if it were just a nomenclature, a list of names for things. Secondly, they assumed the giving of names to things in the world was a simple task, which couldn't be further from the truth.

Moore: What did your mentor, another Robert, think?

Locke: Robert Boyle! He was a leading writer of your second Book, the Book of Nature, whilst also being very knowledgeable about the first. You should read his book, *Seraphic Love*. Robert was clear. He spelt out his anti-Adamic view in *The Excellence of Theology*.

Moore: Indeed he did. I have a passage from it here. It runs:

> I will not urge the received opinion of divines that before the Fall … Adam's knowledge was such that he was able at first sight to give each of the beasts a name expressive of its nature; because I could never find, in spite of some skill in the holy tongue, that the Hebrew names of animals mentioned in the beginning of Genesis argued a clearer insight into their natures than did the names of the same or other animals in Greek or other languages.

That makes it pretty clear he was firmly rejecting words themselves as a path to promoting natural knowledge. The Royal Society's motto, 'Nullius in Verba' spelt out the path the Fellows were determined to follow.

Locke: 'Take nobody's word for it'. 'Nullius in Verba'.

Moore: Absolutely, 'Take nobody's word for it'. You Fellows of the Royal Society believed observation, conjecture and experiment, not the verbal pronouncements of authorities, offered a better way to advance our knowledge of the world.

Locke: Yes, that was our guiding light. My own objection to the Adamic view was actually much more fundamental than Robert Boyle's.

Moore: Go on.

Locke: I believe it is the arbitrary nature of the relation between word and object, between signifier and signified, that ultimately undermines the view of Adam as the great originator of language.

Moore: 'Signifier' and 'signified'! Have you been reading my English copy of the Swiss linguist, Ferdinand de Saussure's *Cours de Linguistique Générale*?

Locke: Yes. I have in fact. I think he shares some of my views, though he sees their significance differently. However, we profoundly differ on others.

Moore: Did you know that Saussure never actually wrote the *Cours*?

Locke: What do you mean?

Moore: The *Cours* was published posthumously. It was written up from notes of two former students, Charles Bally and Albert Sechehaye, who had attended a series of lectures Saussure gave in Geneva, 1910–1911, as far as I remember.

Locke: So we don't know exactly what Saussure said.

Moore: We know approximately.

Locke: Which is of course all we generally know of the writings of earlier authors.

Moore: But to cut to the chase. Which of his views do you share?

Locke: Those of his views that essentially rebut the Adamic view of the origins of language. They're clearest I think in his first two Principles. Principle I: The Arbitrary Nature of the Sign. Principle II: The Linear Nature of the Signifier. I do, however, believe he misses their fundamental significance for the use of language, particularly on Principle II, the question of linearity.

Moore: Shall we come back to that later. Let's consider first the arbitrary nature of the links between words and meanings. Your view certainly distances you from those who, like Robert South, held the Adamic view of the origins of language. For them the link wasn't remotely arbitrary but divinely given. If the Adamic view were right there would be only one language. No Babel. But you thought …

Locke: I thought what I wrote in Book III of *An Essay Concerning Human Understanding*, that we need public words to express our private thoughts, imaginings, feelings. The words that perform that task arise, not by any natural connection between a specific word and a particular idea. But by an arbitrary link between word and idea, between word and imagining, between word and feeling.

Moore: Let me re-phrase that so I'm clear. The role of words is to be marks of ideas and such. And it's the ideas that words mark in our individual heads that are their meaning.

Locke: That's about it. But there's more.

Moore: What more?

Locke: Well, consider the 'common Acceptation' for the meaning of words.

Moore: The meaning we unthinkingly believe we all agree on.

Locke: Exactly, unthinkingly. However much public use brings about a feeling of a 'common Acceptation', there's something that's too easily forgotten.

Moore: Subjectivity.

Locke: Yes. The subjectivity, the inherent indeterminacy of meaning that we keep coming back to in our conversations. Because of the way each of us individually has to grow meanings for words, there is bound to be, in the last resort, a private, subjective element to our meanings. That subjectivity is particularly apparent, as we have already seen, in the different ways in which we understand what I call 'general terms': words like 'justice', or words for emotions such as 'love'.

Moore: It sounds as though it may help to recall your fundamental insight: Words don't mean, individuals mean by way of words.

Locke: That's about it. But there's even more.

Moore: Even more?

Locke: Do you remember Saussure's diagram of the sign?

Moore: The picture of a tree followed by the word 'tree', and a picture of a handsome horse followed by the word 'horse'.

Locke: That's there, but the important, misleading, diagram is the one illustrating the relation between concept and sound image.

Moore: Word and meaning as you would put it. What's misleading about it?

Locke: Well, look at it.

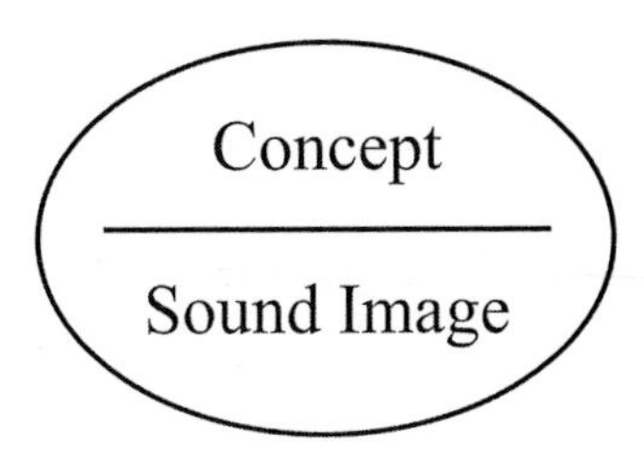

Doesn't it suggest that what the word, the sound image, marks is one concept implying that that concept will be the same for all users of the word? It's far too neat. It's as if Saussure is replacing the false idea of words as a nomenclature inspired by Adam, just a list of things in the world, by the equally false idea of words as a nomenclature of ideas about the world.

Moore: You're right. It's far too tidy. Give me instead your knot and bundle image of the relation between words and their meanings. Saussure's diagram illustrates an entirely different relation, one exactly the opposite of your position.

Locke: Precisely. I have tried to convince you that for me the word, the knot, ties a bundle of ideas, or concepts, which may partly overlap, partly be different from the bundle of ideas it marks for you.

Moore: Don't worry. I am convinced.

Locke: Saussure is right, of course, about the arbitrariness of the links between words and ideas, but fails, as I see it, to follow through on the consequences.

Moore: The chief consequence being of course that the same word can tie different bundles in different minds and different bundles in the same mind at different times.

Locke: Exactly.

Moore: You did say you also had concerns about his Principle II: The Linear Nature of the Signifier.

Locke: Again he's right of course. Language is inescapably linear. But it is the significance of that linearity that Saussure, as I read him, misses.

Moore: What do you think he misses?

Locke: Let me digress briefly so as to answer properly. I've been reading an essay of Condillac's I found on your shelves.

Moore: That must be Condillac's *Essai sur l'origine des connaissances humaines*, 1746.

Locke: That's it. I suspect Condillac and I would have got on famously. He says things I might have said.

Moore: For example?

Locke: Listen to this. 'We never step outside ourselves, and we never perceive anything but our own private thoughts.' Doesn't that sound like me?

Moore: That focus on the private and the subjective does, I agree, have resonances with sentences of yours in Book III of the *Essay*, except Condillac perhaps is more emphatic. The general thrust though is certainly Lockeian.

Locke: How often did I say, 'Words in their primary or immediate Signification, stand for nothing, but the Ideas in the Mind of him that uses them'?

Moore: Repeatedly. We could have used Condillac's sentence as an epigraph for one of our earlier conversations.

Locke: Do you mean the one on an untenable dualism – objective versus subjective. You're right. Condillac would I'm sure deny the possibility of total objectivity.

Moore: But I believe he would have approved of the spectrum of subjectivity we talked about. Where did Condillac stand on Principle II: Linearity?

Locke: More or less where I stood. But he tells a better story.

Moore: Go on, I like stories.

Locke: Well, you'll recall Condillac was at one time tutor to the young Prince of Parma. To drive home the importance of linearity, Condillac stood the lad in front of a shuttered window. He then briefly opened the shutters to give the Prince a view of the landscape. After closing the shutters Condillac asked him to describe what he had seen. Inevitability the Prince was forced into analysing the scene he'd briefly seen into chunks of linear language. What Condillac was doing was driving home the critical distinction between perceiving and talking about what is perceived. In short, he was showing by demonstration that while perception is holistic, speech is linear.

Moore: Saussure certainly didn't follow through on the significance of Principle II for the use of language. You're right of course. In using language we can't help but decompose into parts what our senses deliver as a whole.

Locke: And those parts are decomposed into other parts, and those parts into other parts, offering by way of re-composition endless creativity. I'm indebted to Condillac for sharpening up my understanding of the significance of the inescapable linearity of language. Perception is holistic, speech linear.

Moore: You may be pleased to know he said he was indebted to you, in particular for your *An Essay Concerning Human Understanding*.

Locke: I'm pleased, very pleased.

Moore: You said earlier that, apart from Saussure's Principle I on the arbitrary nature of the links between words and ideas, and his Principle II on Linearity, your view of what students of language should be studying differed profoundly from his. What difference do you have in mind?

Locke: That's easy. I think the difference is encapsulated in the opening sentence of his Chapter V. Pass me the *Cours* and I'll read it to you. Thanks. It runs: 'My definition of language presupposes the exclusion of everything that is outside its organism or system – in a word, of everything known as 'external linguistics.' Among the aspects he excluded implicitly was the very one that concerned me most – words, their meanings, and how far we can hope to understand each other.

Moore: How ironic. The so-called Father of Modern Linguistics sets aside from his concerns the nature, use and signification of language. Small wonder there has been little Lockeian linguistics. Still I've learnt a great deal from you, and not just about the arbitrary nature of the sign. Till next time.

EPILOGUE

'It will possibly be censured as a great piece of Vanity, or Insolence in me, to pretend to instruct this our knowing Age; ... when I own that I publish this Essay with hopes it may be useful to others.'

The Epistle to the Reader
An Essay Concerning Human Understanding

Moore: I have a 'What If ...'

Locke: What's your 'What If'?

Moore: What if 'Secret Reference' were no longer a secret? What if we told the world and people really got it? What if it became recognised as a key element in how we communicate? What would the outcome be? Wouldn't we misunderstand each other less? Might we even understand each other better?

Locke: Dreamer! Starry-eyed idealist! Tell me, how long has *An Essay Concerning Human Understanding* been in print?

Moore: Three centuries and counting.

Locke: Have there been any recent editions?

Moore: Several. Among the best to my mind is one edited and introduced by P.H. Nidditch.

Locke: And has a hungry reading public fallen on Book III, devouring 'Secret Reference'? Made it the anchor of their attempts to understand one another, to understand the language of the world around them, their political world, their religious world, their economic world?

Moore: Admittedly, Book III has not yet set the academic, philosophical or linguistic worlds on fire, nor the general reader of works on language. But I can think of two independent thinkers who, if they'd read it, would have cherished Book III. Both, alas, dead.

Locke: Who do you have in mind?

Moore: Well, you and Jespersen would have got on like a house on fire.

Locke: Otto Jespersen, the great Dane, author of *The Philosophy of Grammar*. I've seen his book on your shelves.

Moore: Consider that book's epigraph. It runs: 'The essence of language is human activity – activity on the part of one individual to make himself understood by another, and activity on the part of that other to understand what was in the mind of the first.'

Locke: Perfect. The focus is exactly where it needs to be, on the individual, the content of their mind, and the activity involved in trying to get across that content to other minds whose exact content is uncertain. I must go back to Jespersen. Remind me where he is.

Moore: Third shelf down, on the right.

Locke: But is that epigraph widely known? Is it treated as a fundamental truth in manuals for improving our ability to communicate clearly?

Moore: Unfortunately not – as far as I know.

Locke: So why should you think your book of our conversations – what are you calling it, *Understanding Misunderstanding: Locke Holds the Key* – why should your efforts fare any better?

Moore: We have to keep trying. And I have the advantage of having translated your ideas into a modern idiom. I hope I've made 'Secret Reference' less of a secret.

Locke: You mentioned two thinkers you thought might have been drawn to Book III, if they'd discussed it. Who was the second?

Moore: Michael Polanyi, radiologist and philosopher of language and mind. I'd like to know what you think of his 1958 book, *Personal Knowledge*. It's also on the third shelf. The title is a fair clue to its contents. Its focus on tacit knowing should resonate with you, given you were once the leading figure on the subjectivity of knowledge!

Locke: I'll put Polanyi at the top of my list. But I'm still puzzled. Why do you dream about the future prospects of the world really understanding 'Secret Reference'? The record suggests it will remain a pearl hidden in the bushes of neglect.

Moore: Not when people fully realise how potent it can be. Believe me, it's made a real difference to me. Since I've taken 'Secret Reference' to heart I've understood more, misunderstood less.

Locke: True. You, currently, are my best student. But, let's face it, who are you? A mover and shaker in the world? The head you're shaking tells me you know you're not.

Moore: Alright, you've made your point. Why should people listen to me? So where does this leave us?

Locke: Where we always are. Trying to make ourselves heard above the babel of confused tongues.

Moore: I agree. We'll have to shout pretty loud to have a chance of being heard.

Locke: But suppose we had a secret weapon.

Moore: A secret weapon! As well as 'Secret Reference'!

Locke: It's coming back to me. Do you recall a way forward you suggested in our very first conversation?

Moore: No, I don't remember. Remembering things is not my strong point these days.

Locke: What you suggested was introducing our, your, book to young people, bringing its ideas into the schools. Make the discussion of words and meanings, degrees of understanding, the tacit, communal conspiracy we enter into in trying to understand each other, a regular part of the curriculum.

Moore: Exciting thought. I can imagine a course – there'd have to be well-chosen examples – so young people could see the way words and meanings actually work. And, moreover, how easily misunderstandings can arise. They might then begin to apply it to their own lives. They might even discover language's dark secret.

Locke: Remind me. What are you calling language's dark secret?

Moore: That words themselves don't contain meanings.

Locke: To discover that, we would need to get their teachers interested. Teachers are important people, very important. They can open minds, sow seeds. Teachers of English for example might find my insights into the links between words and ideas helpful in clarifying the differences in understanding students show.

Moore: You're thinking of when their students are grappling with, say, poetry.

Locke: Exactly. And teachers of a foreign language might be willing to add an arrow to their quiver by not only teaching a language, but also teaching about language.

Moore: You're right. The distinction between knowing a language and knowing about language is vital. When I'm introduced as a linguist, I'm invariably asked, 'How many languages do you speak?' I appear to reflect and then answer: one. The laughter is only dispelled when I introduce the distinction between 'knowing a language' and 'knowing about language'. But do you really think our book could influence work in the classroom?

Locke: Why not? If we can catch the young before their minds get too firmly set!

Moore: We could contact SAPERE.

Locke: Who's he?

Moore: He's not a 'he', it's an organisation, SAPERE's an acronym. It stands for**:** Society for the Advancement of Philosophical Enquiry and Reflection in Education.

Locke: The acronym's well-chosen. From the Latin, 'sapere', to 'know', be 'aware'.

Moore: We still have 'sapient', 'deeply wise', not used very often!

Locke: What's this SAPERE's aim exactly?

Moore: In essence it's to promote philosophically enquiring minds in children. There's some evidence that courses in thinking philosophically have a ripple effect, improving young people's performance in other subjects.

Locke: You think the young could be guided to approach language philosophically, be got to grasp the crucial distinction between what words do and what meanings are?

Moore: Easily! If it were done not abstractly but by illustration, by examples, by instances taken from the language in the classroom. It's children after all who ask the big questions – 'What holds the sky up?', 'Why doesn't it fall?', 'How did language begin?', perhaps later: 'What's the meaning of life?', 'How should I live?', 'Where do I start?' – yet somehow as we grow up we seem to forget to ask. Of course …

Locke: Of course what?

Moore: Of course to get teachers sowing these seeds we would need to think about where the teachers that teach young people are taught.

Locke: Where are teachers trained?

Moore: In a number of places with different names: departments of education, institutes of education, faculties of education, colleges.

Locke: So within these institutions you'd have teachers becoming skilled in discussing the implications of 'Secret Reference', of approaching language philosophically?

Moore: Exactly. And also discussing your ideas on the essential privateness of meanings, on the need to understand our inescapable subjectivity, on recognising the inherent indeterminacy of meanings.

Locke: You're right. By expanding their own horizons they would be well equipped to help students understand both understanding and misunderstanding. Future generations might reap a linguistic harvest! By exploring the ramifications of 'Secret Reference' there's a chance they would've got to grips with – how did your Jespersen put it – the complexity of 'the activity on the part of one individual to make himself understood by another.'